A Time for Hope

*One New York Pastor's Biblical
Response to 9/11, Terrorism and Islam*

One New York Pastor's Biblical
Response to 9/11, Terrorism and Islam

A Time *for* Hope

DAVID EPSTEIN

ANM
publishers

A TIME *for* HOPE

One New York Pastor's Biblical Response to 9/11, Terrorism and Islam

© 2011 by David Epstein

ISBN: 978-0-9715346-5-0 Paperback

Published by:

ANM
publishers
Advancing Native Missions
P.O. Box 5303
Charlottesville, VA 22905
www.adnamis.org

I have known David Epstein for many years as a sensitive and caring pastor who has a wonderful ministry at Calvary Baptist in New York. We can only imagine his shock and horror when the terrorism of 9/11 happened in his beloved city. What you hold in your hands is David's sermons, admonitions and reflections shared with a congregation that was personally affected by this terrible tragedy. You will also read testimonies of God's faithfulness in the midst of fear and terror. Best of all, David emphasizes that Jesus walks with us in the midst of our fears, for our Savior also experienced the terror of crucifixion at the hands of evil men.

Dr. Erwin Lutzer, *Senior Pastor*
The Moody Church, Chicago, Illinois

DEDICATION

This book is dedicated to my dad, Aaron Epstein (Eppie), the finest man I ever knew. He has been with God for about nine years now — because of the love of his Savior Jesus Christ.

His grandfather was a Russian Jew who was persecuted during the pogroms and came to America to find freedom and opportunity for himself and his family. He experienced terrorism first hand. Years later my dad, still a teenager, served in World War II and helped defeat the Nazi terror and rid the world of Hitler. He was a wonderful husband to his wife, Joan, and a great dad to me and my sisters, Kathie Lee and Michie. He was also a loving grandfather and a friend to many.

Dad, you always encouraged me to:

- ✦ Be a man
- ✦ Work hard
- ✦ Think for myself
- ✦ Tell the truth
- ✦ And make you proud
- ✦ (And if possible — write some books!)

This one's for you!

PREFACE

It looked like a scene from Beirut or Kabul: a long line of refugees, dusty, frightened, in shock, semi-lifeless. But it was not the Middle East—it was 57th Street in New York City, as the "refugees" escaped north, a few miles from Ground Zero. Some were members of our own congregation, who had escaped the Twin Towers from as high up as the 87th floor. And we, along with hundreds of churches, had the privilege of offering spiritual, emotional and physical help—the love of God.

In the days and weeks following the terror of 9/11, as we opened the church for prayer and comfort, we experienced a number of divine encounters. On one memorable day, right after the first anthrax scare in NYC, a young professional woman entered the sanctuary right off 57th Street. She was focused and excited as she exclaimed to me and to an assistant pastor, "Please help me to find God today. I can't go home before I know God." We then had the joy of sharing God's love for her in Jesus Christ. She bowed her head and prayed, acknowledging her sin and asking God's forgiveness, expressing the desire to give her life to God and to follow Jesus Christ. She left joyful, confident and enthusiastic about her new life in Christ—just one more living example of how God produces beauty out of ashes.

We live in an unprecedented time of spiritual opportunity. God is drawing many hearts to himself in this time of loss, anger, fear and uncertainty, all because God's love and power are greater than the evil around us. In this battle for the minds and souls of men and women, may we be found faithful, knowing that God has called us to his kingdom *"for such a time as this."* (Esther 4:14)

Pastor Dave Epstein
Calvary Baptist Church
New York City

CONTENTS

INTRODUCTION

Friday, September 7, 2001—the Friday before 9/11—was a beautiful, yet strange day. My wife, Sandy, and I had spent two wonderful weeks on vacation visiting our son, Josh, his wife, Richelle, and our newborn granddaughter, Kyler, in Pennsylvania and then our son, Jason, his wife, Amanda, and our newborn grandson, Elijah, in Western Canada.

I was flying back to New York City that day looking forward to beginning my fifth year as the senior pastor of Calvary Baptist Church in midtown Manhattan. Sandy was going to remain a few more days before flying to Ontario to teach some women's conferences and later rejoin me in New York. I was really looking forward to being with my own congregation and preaching in my own pulpit after a few weeks of summer conference ministry and vacation. But I was also feeling unsettled as I flew home. It was strange, I thought to myself—I have no word from the Lord about what I should preach this Sunday or any Sunday for that matter.

Normally, by the end of each summer's ministry and vacation, the Lord would have clearly directed me to the next series of messages I should preach—but the Lord was silent. So I advised my executive assistant that I would be preaching a communion message on September the 9th and I would trust the Lord for further direction. Then, on a gorgeous, blue, cloudless, surreal Tuesday morning, September 11th, two planes crashed into the two World Trade Center towers in New York City transforming them into towering infernos. As my staff and I scrambled to open the church and check on our people who worked in the World Trade Center, I whispered to God, *Lord, now I know why you were silent—why I had no word and direction about what to preach this fall. You knew what was coming—and now you want me to preach to my people, and join others in preaching to this city "for such a time as this."*

As my staff and I plunged into the work of caring for and encouraging scared and hurting people, which for me included preparing to preach five days later, it really hit me that 9/11 was by far the greatest challenge and opportunity I had ever faced in my 29 years of ministry. This next sermon was also the most difficult and demanding message I had ever given. What do you say in the midst of such evil and suffering?

We were told that the sermon would be carried live in England because so many British citizens had died in the towers. Calvary Baptist Church was known to many in Great Britain because one of my distinguished predecessors, Dr. Stephen Olford, an internationally respected preacher and evangelist, had come to New York City from a pastorate in England.

But no word came from God. Each day, as I waited on the Lord, the silence grew more deafening and my anxiety and heaviness grew. Then Saturday morning, September 15th, the Lord graciously broke through. I had been reading various passages in the gospels and began thinking about the phone calls many of those trapped in the Trade Center had made to their loved ones in their last moments of life. They would say things like, "There's been an explosion—fire is everywhere—I'm trapped—I may not make it out—hug the children for me—I love you." And then silence.

I thought of Jesus on the cross. In a way it was his tower. And yet he had gone there willingly—to die for us all. And while on the 105th floor of his cross, his tower, he had made a number of calls also—seven calls—last calls. And with each call he offered hope to those suffering the evil, death and tragedy of 9/11. And he offers hope to you also.

The purpose of this book is to inspire hope in the face of terrorism. For this to happen we must think biblically about 9/11, terrorism and

Islam. There are other important perspectives, of course—the political, sociological, psychological, historical, and religious—but the focus here is biblical. Don't be too quick to write such a perspective off. At its root, religious terrorism is a deadly plague. Hate and murder are the poisonous byproducts of a diseased spirituality, morality and ideology. Therefore, Islamic terrorism cannot be defeated by military, political and economic means alone—they are absolutely necessary but not sufficient! Truth is also required—spiritual and moral truth and a discerning worldview. The Bible has proven for 3500 years that it knows a little something about such things! The Apostle Paul, formerly known as the terrorist Saul, knows better than anyone the formula for ultimately defeating terrorism:

> For though we live in the world, we do not wage war as the world does. The weapons we fight with are not the weapons of the world. On the contrary, they have divine power to demolish strongholds. We demolish arguments and every pretension that sets itself up against the knowledge of God, and we take captive every thought to make it obedient to Christ. (2 Cor. 10:3-5)

A biblical perspective will equip us to better understand Islam and to wage "total war"—not against the Muslim people, but against terrorism.

The book's first four chapters are entitled *A Time for Hope*, *A Time for War*, *A Time to Heal*, and *A Time for Peace*. These are the four messages I shared with my congregation in New York City on the four Sundays following 9/11. They focus on the power of the gospel to give hope in the darkest days.

Chapter 5, *Confessions of a Terrorist*, helps us understand what makes a religious terrorist tick! It is a journey into the mind of a terrorist, the Pharisee Saul, before he encountered Jesus Christ and became the Apostle Paul. His story is gripping and extremely relevant as we confront terrorism today. Paul helps us understand how a terrorist thinks, what he feels, and why he does what he does! It is both enlightening and terrifying! Paul shocks us with the truth that the most effective weapon against hate and murder is the love and power of God!

A Time *for* Hope

Chapters 6-9, entitled *A Biblical Look at Islam,* take us into the world of Allah, Mohammad, the Koran and Jihad. These are messages I preached within weeks of 9/11 because, tragically, it was a teachable moment. They address important questions: Are the God of the Bible and the God of Islam the same God? Who is the greater prophet—Jesus or Mohammad? Is the Bible or the Koran God's final written revelation? How do men and women get right with God—by God's grace or by human effort? The answers to these questions are vital in understanding, loving and reaching Muslims and in confronting and defeating Islamic terrorism.

At Calvary Baptist Church in New York City as we worshipped and served God together in the days following the tragedy and as we heard and responded to God's Word—we began to hope again.

PART I

9/11

CHAPTER I
A Time for Hope

SUNDAY, SEPTEMBER 16, 2001

Our president has said, "Barbarians have declared war on the United States—we are at war." Until last Tuesday, the greatest single loss of American lives in one day took place in September of 1862 at the Battle of Antietam. That day 4700 Americans lost their lives...brother slaughtering brother. It was so horrific that President Lincoln said at the time, quoting our Lord Jesus Christ, "A house divided against itself cannot stand." (Matthew 12:25) More lives may have been lost on 9/11 than on any single day in the history of the United States of America—with one huge difference: Today we are one nation...one nation united.

Is it a coincidence that you and I are here in New York City, from every state and every nation in the year of our Lord 2001, for such a time as this? No. Was it a coincidence that God raised up Winston Churchill with all his blood, sweat, toil and tears to be the Prime Minister of Britain during World War II? No. Was it a coincidence that FDR was the President of the United States during the titanic struggle against the Nazis? No. Is it a coincidence that God has his people here, in his sovereign purpose and will, for such a time as this? No. We are all here in the will and in the calling of Almighty God. United!

A Time *for* Hope

Islamic terrorists attacked the symbols of America's financial and military strength when they targeted the World Trade Center and the Pentagon. But in reality their greatest hatred is reserved for our political freedom, our religious faith expressed in our Judeo-Christian heritage, and our friend and ally, the nation Israel. America was founded on faith in the living God—the God of Abraham, Isaac, and Jacob; God the Father, Son and Holy Spirit. To topple a nation whose God is the Lord—you must topple the Lord himself. And that will never happen! Never...

There was a prophet in Israel named Jeremiah; he was called the weeping prophet. When he saw the suffering and agony of the Jewish people and the destruction of their temple in Jerusalem, he asked a poignant question, "The summer is passed, and the harvest is ended, and we are not saved. Is there no balm in Gilead? Is there no physician there? Is there no healing for the daughter of my people?" (Jeremiah 8:22) Six hundred years later, a prophet greater than Jeremiah left Bethany and ascended the Mount of Olives and then descended to the Garden of Gethsemane—and as he looked out over the city of Jerusalem, he wept over it. God is weeping over New York City today. But God's love is greater than evil; and God's power is greater than terrorism. And the hope God gives his people is brighter than this present darkness.

As I watched Billy Graham ascend the steps of the pulpit of the National Cathedral, he was clearly a man frail in body but strong in spirit. He needed to be assisted to the pulpit, but then the power of God came upon him and he said, "I am an old man now. But the older I get, the more I hold on to the hope I first received as a young man so many years ago." As he spoke my mind returned to the cross, to the last calls of Jesus, to the only place we find real and lasting hope.

Between 9 a.m. on that Good Friday morning when Jesus was crucified, until 3 p.m. when he died he made seven calls.

Hope For Forgiveness

The very first call Jesus made was to his Father, and he offered an amazing prayer, a special request; "Father forgive them for they do not know what they are doing." (Luke 23:34) I don't want to start here—our nation doesn't want to start here—but it's where Jesus started at 9 a.m. on that Good Friday morning.

In his very first call, Jesus said that even in the midst of the evil, murder and suffering of 9/11 there is hope for forgiveness. Do you mean the possibility of forgiveness for vicious terrorists who are still on the run and at war with America? Yes! I am a proud and grateful American citizen, but first of all a follower of Jesus Christ. I also was disgusted as I saw footage of terrorist sympathizers dancing with joy in the West Bank, in Gaza, and in various Muslim capitals around the world as they received the news of 9/11. Closer to home, they celebrated in Ottawa, Ontario, Canada, a city I preached in for 7 years. There were also celebrations in Newark, New Jersey, just across the Hudson River from the carnage in New York City. Father, forgive them? You really mean you want to see Osama Bin Laden come under conviction from God for his evil crimes and to repent of his sins and confess Jesus as his Lord and Savior and to be forgiven? Yes! I want every terrorist to repent and be transformed by the love and mercy of God—even as they face human justice. I believe this knowing that in my own church family and circle of friends some lost loved ones to the terrorists.

One woman in our church lost her precious granddaughter, and one of our friends lost her wonderful husband, while pregnant with their first child. We also have friends who escaped the towers. We have some young people in our church, who while at school watched people jumping to their deaths from the burning towers leaving horrible images in their minds and hearts. Can I really pray, "Lord bring every terrorist to genuine grief and sorrow over their wickedness and evil? Do a major work by your Holy Spirit in their hearts, and bring them to the foot of the cross of Jesus Christ where they will find God's forgiveness—even as they face man's judgment?" After all, that's also where another notorious terrorist found his forgiveness.

You remember a Jewish Pharisee named Saul who believed he was serving God 2,000 years ago when he hunted down every Christian he could find—men, women and children—and arrested them and even had some of them executed. One day while on the Damascus Road in Syria, in the midst of one of his murderous missions, Saul encountered Jesus Christ and received forgiveness at that same cross—and the terrorist became a champion of the love and mercy of God.

Forgiveness is hard. Jesus said following him was never going to be easy; therefore, the first call Jesus made from the cross—the only call he made for the first three hours on the cross—was for forgiveness. If we don't begin there—we can never begin.

HOPE FOR PARADISE

Jesus made a second call that day, in which he made a sacred promise, which is also recorded in Luke 23. The message of forgiveness had a profound effect on one of the two men who died next to him. In verse 42 this man made a personal request to Jesus, "Lord, remember me when you come into your kingdom." And Jesus responded, "Truly I say to you, today you shall be with me in paradise."(vs. 43)

We've been hearing a lot about paradise in the midst of the war on terror. Islamic terrorists preach to their young recruits that if they die while fighting the enemies of Islam in jihad, particularly while killing Jews and Americans, they will immediately enter paradise and enjoy 72 virgin brides and many other rewards for their martyrdom. In powerful contrast, Jesus says you don't get to paradise by killing God's enemies; you get to paradise by loving and trusting God's son, who then empowers you to love your neighbor as yourself.

The Pharisee Saul, who became the apostle Paul, was a former terrorist who learned this truth and had a radical transformation. It's interesting to note that the thief who trusted Jesus had been ridiculing and blaspheming him up until just before noon on that Good Friday morning. Both Matthew and Mark reveal that both criminals who were crucified next to Jesus had been his adversaries even while dying next to Him. But something powerful happened. The message of forgiveness that Jesus shared over a three-hour period began to impact one of the condemned men. The scripture says:

> Then one of the criminals who were hanged blasphemed him saying, "If you are the Christ, save yourself and us." But the other answering rebuked him, saying, "Do you not even fear God seeing you are under the same condemnation?" (Luke 23:39-40)

This one man began to experience a fear and reverence for God that he did not have earlier. Then he added in verse 41, "We are punished justly, for we are getting what our deeds deserve." He admitted his guilt and realized his punishment was just. Clearly it was the message of forgiveness which worked this godly fear and conviction of sin in his heart. And then he concluded in verse 41, referring to Jesus, "But this man has done nothing wrong." He realized that Jesus, in contrast to himself and his partner in crime, was just and innocent and undeserving of death. When God uses the cross of forgiveness to inspire someone to fear God, to recognize and admit sin, and to acknowledge the innocence of Jesus—the result is life-transforming, "Lord, remember me when you come into your kingdom." It is at the cross that we find forgiveness and the promise of life after death; the promise of paradise.

The cross was ground zero. The cross was God's holy war against sin, death, hell, Satan, and human evil and depravity. The cross was God's holy war against every form of racial, sexual, political, religious, and ethnic terrorism. We honor and remember each one whose life was taken so suddenly by Islamic terrorists on 9/11; and we thank God for the continuing hope that those who died loving and trusting in Jesus Christ have also heard and embraced the promise—"You shall be with me in paradise."

HOPE FOR JUSTICE

Jesus made a third call from his tower, the cross, just before 3 pm, in which he cried out a heart wrenching question, recorded in Matthew 27:46, "My God, My God, why have you forsaken me?" And with that cry Jesus teaches us that at the cross there is hope for justice. What Jesus agonized over was why his Father would utterly abandon him and leave him desolate and alone. Good question. And the answer is that God was pouring out his

A TIME *for* HOPE

justice on his innocent son. God was satisfying all the demands of his holiness through the substitutionary death of Jesus for my sins, and for yours, and for the sins of the whole world. Jesus became a sin offering on the cross—so that guilty people like you and me can receive God's forgiveness and mercy—because Jesus the innocent one "became sin for us" and took God's holy and just wrath upon Himself. The cross was a cry for justice.

As Americans we know that there are two vital aspects to justice. The first is that everyone has the presumption of innocence until proven guilty in a court of law. The first side of justice, as we hear Jesus cry for justice, is that we protect the innocent, whatever race or ethnic group or religion they may be. Justice always protects the innocent! Therefore, if we individually or collectively as a nation target, revile, and attack any man, woman or child just because they are a Muslim, or Arab, or both as in the case of 9/11—we dishonor and disobey God and violate divine justice. Remember, it was one of our own who bombed Oklahoma City. The evil is also among us. And we did not go out and arrest every young man who had fought in the Gulf War because of the evil actions of Timothy McVeigh.

At Columbine it was our children who were the terrorists and the victims of terrorism. Eric Harris and Dylan Klebold were American terrorists full of evil and murder. They slaughtered their classmates indiscriminately. We didn't go out and hunt down and arrest every teenager in Colorado for the crimes of these two young murderers. Genuine justice protects the innocent.

The second vital aspect to justice is that genuine justice also punishes the wicked and the guilty. How is this punishment to be administered? Not by personal vengeance, but by God himself, through the agency of government. The Apostle Paul, in his letter to the Romans, distinguishes between ungodly personal vengeance and righteous divine justice. In Romans 12:17-21, he argues that there is no place for personal vengeance in the pursuit of justice:

> Repay no one evil for evil. Have regard for good things in the
> sight of all men. If it is possible, as much as depends on you,
> live peaceably with all men. Beloved, do not avenge your-

selves, but rather give place to wrath; for it is written, "Vengeance is mine, I will repay says the Lord." Therefore, if your enemy hungers, feed him, if he thirsts, give him a drink; for in so doing you will heap coals of fire on his head. Do not be overcome by evil, but overcome evil with good.

So if God forbids revenge, but promises his own brand of justice, how does he do it? In Romans 13 God tells us that he has given government the responsibility and authority to pursue justice:

Let every soul be subject to the governing authorities. For there is no authority except from God, and the authorities that exist are appointed by God. Therefore whoever resists the authority resists the ordinance of God, and those who resist will bring judgment on themselves. For rulers are not a terror to good works, but to evil. Do you want to be unafraid of the authority? Do what is good, and you will have praise from the same. For he is God's minister to you for good. But if you do evil, be afraid; for he does not bear the sword in vain; for he is God's minister, an avenger to execute wrath on him who practices evil.

That is why God gives government the power of capital punishment and the right to pursue a just war, so that evil might be punished. President Bush said, "This conflict was begun on the timing and the terms of others. It will end in a way and at an hour of our own choosing. Those who make war against the United States have chosen their own destruction." And Jesus said, "Those who live by the sword will die by the sword." (Matthew 26:52) There is hope for justice!

HOPE FOR LOVED ONES

Jesus made a fourth call from the tower that day. And this one was to his mom. The apostle John tells us that:

...near the cross of Jesus stood his mother and his mother's sister, Mary, the wife of Clopas and Mary Magdalene. And when Jesus saw his mother there, and the disciple whom he loved, he said to his mother, "Dear woman, behold your son." And he said to John his disciple, "Behold your mother." And from that hour that disciple took her to his home. (John 19:25-27)

In his own loving and caring way, Jesus was saying to his mom that he was not going to get off the cross alive and that he loved her and would take care of her. The cross had become a place of hope for his family and for yours.

When Jesus was eight days old, thirty-three years before he died on that cross, his earthly father, Joseph, and his mother, Mary, dedicated him at the temple. There, a man named Simeon gave a prophecy concerning the baby Jesus. Luke 3:34-35 states:

Then Simeon blessed them, and said to Mary his mother, "Behold this child is destined for the fall and rising of many in Israel, and for a sign which will be spoken against (yes, a sword will pierce through your own soul also), that the thoughts of many hearts may be revealed."

The cruel death of her firstborn son was the sword piercing Mary's soul. She watched her son die right in front of her eyes! Yet he died loving and caring for her right to the bitter end.

There are many people who have lost friends and loved ones because of the evil of 9/11. Many others are still missing. This grips me—hope for families—hope for loved ones. Jesus says he will not leave us as orphans. He will come to us. In that personal way we need him most, he is with us. That's why his name is Immanuel—God is with us. Even as we pray for those still missing, we also pray for their desperate and hurting families. We pray that God would bless each family and meet every need with his power, love and comfort.

Hope in Weakness

He made a fifth call from the cross, his tower, immediately after caring for his mother. The scripture tells us that Jesus, "knowing that all was now complete, so that the scripture would be fulfilled said, 'I am thirsty." (John 19:18) He said in effect, I am human—I am God in the flesh but I am fully human and I am exhausted. I am in agony and I am so thirsty, I can't bear it. Someone, please give me a drink. He made his fifth call saying there is hope in weakness. We are also weak and vulnerable. Rescuers are still working frantically to find those who may still be buried alive. We can hear their cries this morning in New York City—"Lord, I am so thirsty in here. I can't breathe. I can't get any water. I am so parched." And the rescuers themselves, as brave and courageous as they are, are also exhausted and thirsty. And the volunteers feeding and giving them drinks and showing the love of God to them are also aware of their own weakness. Loved ones and family members and friends of those yet to be found are also desperate and fearful, saying—"God I'm thirsty too, I need a touch from you; I am thirsty for some sign of hope." And God says—"I give hope in weakness."

What chance does human flesh and blood have against raging fire and collapsing concrete and steel? How do our hearts and minds survive the terror and despair and anxiety and fear? But God says that he will strengthen us—that his power will be perfected in our weakness. God tells us that when we are weak, then we are strong because of Him. (2 Corinthians 12:9-10) God bless New York's bravest and New York's finest. Jesus said it best, "Greater love has no one than this, than to lay down one's life for his friends." (John 15:13)

Hope for Peace

Jesus made a sixth call just before he died at 3 p.m. on Good Friday. In response to his thirst, the scripture says:

> A jar of wine vinegar was there so they soaked a sponge and they
> put the sponge on a stalk of hyssop and lifted it to Jesus' lips.
> And when he had received the drink Jesus said, "It is finished."
> And bowing his head, He gave up his spirit. (John 19:30)

The sixth call was a victory cry—"It is finished." Jesus didn't go to the 105th floor of the World Trade Center, to the cross, saying—Father,

I hope this works. He said, "It is accomplished—it is done." God has reconciled the world to Himself. God has declared a peace treaty with the human race. We declared war on God, but God declared peace on us! God has offered us forgiveness through Jesus Christ—He is our redemption. Therefore we can have peace with God, peace within ourselves, and peace with others. Nations can be at peace with one another because God made peace with us at the cross. Jesus waged war for us at the cross and "by his stripes we are healed." (Isaiah 53:5)

A Muslim cleric from the Middle East communicated with President Bush yesterday and said, "President Bush, if you want peace and security, you need to convert to Islam." But Islam rejects the cross. So how can we have peace with God and with one another without the Prince of Peace? The Camp David Accord and the Oslo Accord were done in good faith, but they failed and will continue to fail. The Calvary Accord, where Jesus waged war and shed his blood to make peace has succeeded once and for all—"It is finished." Today, if you are still without Christ and his love demonstrated in the cross—isn't it wonderful to know he offers you grace and forgiveness once again. Second chances. "God's mercies are new every morning, great is his faithfulness." (Lamentations 3:22-23)

HOPE FOR HEALING

The seventh and last call that Jesus made is recorded in Luke 23, where the calls first began; so we've come full circle. In verse 44 we read:

> It was now about the sixth hour and darkness came over the whole land until the ninth hour for the sun stopped shining and the curtain of the temple was torn in two. Jesus called out with a loud voice, "Father, into your hands I commit my spirit." And having said this, he breathed his last.

Jesus proclaimed with that seventh and last call that there is hope for healing; there's hope for revival; there's hope for renewal. In effect Jesus was saying—Father, the only place I want my spirit to be now is in your hands. And I believe that's exactly what God is calling us to do as New Yorkers and Americans—to put ourselves and our nation into God's hands. God is the only one who can give life to the dead; the only one who can give new life to the living; the only one with the power to regenerate and revive us. Lord Jesus, remember me. Remember us. He is the only one who can save you, forgive you, and set you free. He's the only one who can deliver you from death and hell and judgment. He's the only one who can give you hope and power and meaning and purpose and a future. "Into thy hands I commit my spirit." "Is there no balm in Gilead? Is there no physician there? Is there no healing for the wound of my people?" And the answer is—yes there is. Jesus of Nazareth—he restores my soul. (Psalm 23:3)

There was a man and a family that Jesus loved very much. It was Lazarus and his sisters, Mary and Martha. Most of you know the story. Lazarus died and Jesus delayed coming. And when he came, Martha, who loved Jesus and her brother very much, ran to Jesus and said:

> "Lord, if you had been here, you could have kept this from happening. My brother would not have died." And Jesus said to her, "Your brother Lazarus will rise again." And Martha said, "Lord, we know that he will rise again at the resurrection at the last day." And Jesus said, "Martha, I am the resurrection and I am the life and he who believes in me, though he die, yet shall he live. And he who lives and believes in me will never die. Do you believe this?" And Martha said, "Yes Lord, I believe that you are the Christ, the Son of God who was to come into the world." (John 11:20-28)

Is that the cry of your heart today? I hope it is, because that's the cry of hope.

President Bush read from Romans, Chapter 8, and I want to close triumphantly there:

> And we know that in all things God works for the good of those who love him, who have been called according to his purpose. For those God foreknew he also predestined to be conformed to

the image of his Son, that he might be the firstborn among many brothers and sisters. And those he predestined, he also called; those he called, he also justified; those he justified, he also glorified. What then shall we say in response to these things? If God is for us, who can be against us? He who did not spare his own Son, but gave him up for us all—how will he not also, along with him, graciously give us all things? Who will bring any charge against those whom God has chosen? It is God who justifies. Who then is the one who condemns? No one. Christ Jesus who died—more than that, who was raised to life—is at the right hand of God and is also interceding for us. Who shall separate us from the love of Christ? Shall trouble or hardship or persecution or famine or nakedness or danger or sword? As it is written: "For your sake we face death all day long; we are considered as sheep to be slaughtered." No, in all these things we are more than conquerors through him who loved us. For I am convinced that neither death nor life, neither angels nor demons, neither the present nor the future, nor any powers, neither height nor depth, nor anything else in all creation, will be able to separate us from the love of God that is in Christ Jesus our Lord. (Romans 8:28-39)

In the name of God the Father and God the Son and God the Holy Spirit. Amen.

CHAPTER 2
A Time for War

As we approached the second Sunday after 9/11, my music director said to me, "You'll never believe who we scheduled months ago to provide the special music for this Sunday. It's the West Point Cadet Choir!" I was amazed at the way God had been orchestrating this service. Our former music director, Craig Williams, had left our church just a few months before 9/11 to assume his new duties at West Point, and we had made arrangements with him to return the third Sunday of September with the cadets. And I had also been led by God to preach on the topic — *A Time for War*. The obvious presence of God encouraged me as I began to preach to my people on September 23, 2001...

SUNDAY, SEPTEMBER 23, 2001

What a blessing it is to have the West Point Cadet Choir here with us this morning, and our own Craig Williams, our brother, friend and co-worker for so many years. God tells us to go into all the world and preach the gospel — even in wartime. Even now we must take the gospel to Afghanistan, Iraq and only the Lord knows where else. Islamic terrorists, led by Osama Bin Laden and supported by specific terrorist nations have declared war on the United States. In 1998 Bin Laden signed a fatwah, an Islamic religious decree, calling on Muslims to kill Americans. He was quoted then as saying, "Our enemy, our target, if God gives Muslims the opportunity to do so, is every American male, whether he is directly fighting us or paying taxes."

Obviously, in Bin Laden's mind, the war is not limited to American males. It also includes innocent civilians, men, women and children. Bin Laden is already an indicted international fugitive. Beyond a reasonable doubt he was involved in the 1993 bombing of the World Trade Center. He was also clearly involved in the bombing of the U.S. Embassies in Kenya and Tanzania—which is why he is wanted now. For those who clamor for more evidence, we have the evidence to indict him in other terrorist activities. New evidence is being gathered on his involvement in the latest acts of terrorism, as well as 9/11. It is important to understand that it's terrorists who hate us and want to destroy us. Most Muslims and Arabs are not driven by hatred and terror—it is the Islamic terrorist movement that is our enemy. They hate us for our freedom. They hate us for our democracy. But lets not be naïve, they also hate us for our religious faith.

This is not true for most Muslims, but those involved in terrorism actually hate us because of our Christian and Jewish faith. They refer to us as *infidels* and *unbelievers*. And they also hate us for our love for the Jewish people and our friendship with Israel, as we stand allied with the only democracy in the Middle East. We are hated for many reasons. Therefore, they have declared war on us. America is public enemy #1 for Islamic terrorists. President Bush, our Commander in Chief said, "Barbarians have declared war on the American people. We are at war. This conflict was begun on the timing and terms of others; it will end in a way and at an hour of our choosing. Those who make war against the United States have chosen their own destruction."

I truly believe that it will be necessary for us, as a nation, to destroy Islamic terrorism and its potential to eventually strike us with nuclear, chemical and biological weapons. They have declared war not only on the United States, but on civilization itself. We must destroy Islamic terrorism before it possesses and utilizes the weapons which will destroy everything that is good in this world. Last Sunday, the first Sunday after the horrendous moral perversion and evil of September 11, we talked about a time for hope, and we talked about the cross of Jesus Christ that our brothers and sisters in the West Point Choir have sung about in the two services today; the cross, where we humble ourselves and are spiritually broken before God—and then are healed by him as well. The cross where we find hope, forgiveness, healing and justice. When Jesus cried out, "My God, my God why have you forsaken me," that was a cry for justice. And that's what I want to talk about today. God will now pursue justice through the war on terror. But let's always remember that justice always has two sides. Justice always protects the innocent, regardless of a person's race or ethnicity or religious persuasion.

Justice would never seek to harm innocent Arabs or Muslims because of the evil actions of a few. Justice never takes the law into its own hands as personal vengeance or evil vigilantism. But justice does punish the wicked. So be afraid—be very afraid. Because the Lord God says in his word that he has raised up Caesar. He has ordained human government. He has established nations, to honor what is good and to punish what is evil. God has raised up President Bush and the United States of America. He has raised up West Point, Annapolis and Colorado Springs. He has raised up the military to be his instrument, a servant of God. According to Romans chapter 13, government has the authority and responsibility to reward good and punish evil; therefore the government and military are servants and instruments of God for righteousness and judgment to bring the wrath of God upon the evil-doer. And we thank God that there is a time for justice. There is a time for war.

For Osama Bin Laden it's a holy war. It's jihad. And the rallying cry is "Allahu Akbar—God is great!" But for you and me, our brothers and sisters in the military and President Bush, it's a just war—because every individual and every nation has the right before God to defend their life, their liberty, and their families. It's a *just* war. And God is holy and God is just. So is it also God's war? This is a profound question. I only know this, as a Christian—I believe the Bible, and therefore I believe three things about God and this war:

1. God knows all about it. It hasn't taken him by surprise.

2. God is allowing it in his permissive will.

3. He is using it to fulfill his good, noble and divine purposes that were determined in the eternal secret counsels of God before history ever began.

Let me give you a number of reasons why I believe this is God's war and what God is going to accomplish in it. I am speaking carefully and humbly because of the scriptures, which are the Word of God. This is the only reason why I feel I can speak this way—because of the word that God has given to us.

GOD USES WAR TO JUDGE PEOPLES AND NATIONS

God is using this war to judge peoples and nations. Because God is holy and just, he will use war as an instrument of his judgment. I want you to listen to the prophet Jeremiah. As you read his prophecy, you go back 2600 years—and it's as if nothing has changed in the Middle East. You find the Iraqis warring against the Israelis. Nebuchadnezzar, the forbearer of Saddam Hussein was at war with Israel and the Jews. And in Jeremiah 25:1-11, we find that God judges nations and peoples in war—and sometimes it's his own nation and his own people whom he judges! In verse 8 we read that the Lord God Almighty said to Judah, to Israel:

> Because you have not listened to my words I am going to summon all the peoples of the north and my servant Nebuchadnezzar, and he is going to bring judgment on you.

And three times Babylon attacked...in 605 BC, 597 BC, and 586 BC. In the third military incursion they burned the city and destroyed the great temple of Solomon. I think today of our great nation, America, and our great history—but I also think of times when God has judged us. I especially think of the Civil War, that war that was fought bravely by both sides. And that war, from the Union's perspective, was fought to keep the nation united and to set men and women free from their bonds of slavery.

Thank God for those goals. But I also know that in the Civil War, brothers slaughtered brothers and fathers killed sons on the battlefield. This great nation lost more men in that war—more than 600,000 died—than in all the other American wars together! We must believe that one reason for that horrific carnage was God's judgment on a nation that had brutally enslaved men, women and children for more than 200 years. Americans abused and exploited precious people made in the image of God for whom Christ died. President Lincoln, in the midst of the Civil War, on March 30,1863 called for the nation to pray and fast. He clearly understood the Civil War to be a judgment of God on America for her sins—especially the evil of slavery. So he declared to the American people that:

> ...because we know that nations like individuals, are subjected to punishments and chastisements in this world—may we not justly fear that the awful calamity of civil war, which now desolates the land, may be but a punishment inflicted upon us for our presumptuous sins to the needful end of our national reformation as a whole people. We have been the recipients of the choicest bounties of heaven. We have been preserved, these many years, in peace and prosperity. We have grown in numbers, wealth and power, as no other nation has ever grown...but we have forgotten God. (Senate Resolution, adopted March 3, 1863)

Two years later during his second Inaugural Address on March 4, 1865, President Lincoln was even more graphic in declaring the Civil War to be a judgment of God on America because of slavery:

> If God wills that it (the Civil War) continue until all the wealth piled up by the bondsman's two hundred and fifty years of unrequited toil shall be sunk, and until every drop of blood drawn by the lash shall be paid by another drawn with the sword, as was said three thousand years ago, so still must it be said, "The judgments of the Lord are true and righteous altogether."

A TIME *for* HOPE

God uses war to judge nations! He used pagan Babylon to judge Israel. And then he judged Babylon! In Jeremiah 25:12 God says, "When the 70 years are fulfilled, I am going to punish Babylon." So the Lord punished his own people and then he punished those whom he used to punish his own people! And he punished them big time. God still works this way. Do you remember Dresden and Nuremberg during World War II? The war began with the blitzkrieg into Poland; but it ended with the allied fire bombing of Dresden and the Nuremberg trials. God uses war to judge nations and peoples. We all remember Hiroshima and Nagasaki. The war in the Pacific began with the Japanese attack on Pearl Harbor and ended with an American nuclear strike against Japan. God uses war to judge!

I speak to you today wearing many hats. I am a Christian, a pastor, and an American. I am a man who wishes I had three lives so I could preach the gospel, dig in the rubble of Ground Zero, and chase Bin Laden. I believe as Americans we must strike back at terrorism as hard as we can. I believe we are facing the greatest threat to our freedom and our future since World War II. The threat we face today is even greater than World War II because of the potential for human destruction from nuclear, biological and chemical weapons in the hands of people who value death more than life. I believe if we do not destroy the terrorists wherever they are found—and if we do not defeat terrorism in whatever nation it is found—we will be offering up our children to destruction. I believe the only way we can win this war against Islamic terror is to make every nation and individual involved in the atrocities of 9/11 a target of justice. We need to make the destruction of terrorists such an example of justice that every nation that harbors terrorists will say, "We've got to hunt down and destroy the terrorists in our own country right away because if we don't, and one of them gets loose and does something to the United States—our country, as we know it, may cease to exist." I don't say this as a bloodthirsty person committed to vengeance. I say this as a realist committed to justice. If we don't hit Islamic terrorism hard and turn every terrorist-supporting nation into a terrorist-hunting nation, we have no hope, and neither do our children and grandchildren. I believe this with all my heart. God uses war to punish evil! And now there's only one question to consider—What nation and people is God judging this time?

President Bush began by calling this war a "crusade against terror"—*Operation Infinite Justice*—but he changed those words because they were seen as insensitive to most Muslims who, of course, are not in any way responsible for the terror. But the bottom line is this—God has launched a crusade against terrorism; God is the instrument and author of infinite justice; and he uses nations to judge nations.

It is very quiet in this sanctuary today.

GOD USES WAR TO SET PEOPLE FREE

The second reason the war on terror is God's war is because God uses war to set people free. He uses war to establish liberty and to give life both politically and spiritually. God is a God of love and he will even show his love in the midst of war. He uses war to save, to liberate and to deliver.

The book of Esther is the only book in the Bible where God is not mentioned by name and yet his presence is palpable. And in the book of Esther, in the midst of a war between the Persians and the Jews, we see how God uses warfare to establish freedom. The time of Esther is the 5th century BC and the place is ancient Persia. The Jews were facing a 5th century BC Persian final solution to the Jewish problem—a Holocaust. They were being threatened by the most powerful empire known to man up until that time—the empire of Xerxes the Great which stretched from India to Ethiopia.

Xerxes had married Esther, a Jewish girl, whose Jewish identity was unknown to him. God was working out his sovereign purposes in history by using this Jewish girl to deliver his people from this Persian genocide. Eventually God used Esther to turn the heart of her husband to protect the Jews, instead of destroying them. The edict for their destruction had already been signed by the king and could not be reversed, but the king allowed the Jews to defend themselves on the day of battle. In Esther 8:11 we read:

A TIME *for* HOPE

King Xerxes' edict granted the Jews in every city the right to assemble and protect themselves because an order had been delivered for them to be destroyed.

This was the Middle East all over again 2500 years ago, but this was not Iraq and Israel, as in Jeremiah—but Iran and Israel. Nothing ever changes, does it? Or ever will, until the Messiah changes it one day!

This is the God who punishes nations for their evil and wickedness and also allows nations to wage a just war to protect themselves. The Jews defeated their Persian adversaries—God delivered his people—and in the city of Susah in ancient Persia the Jews had a joyous celebration, a time of happiness, joy, gladness and honor. (Esther 8:15)

The first way God sets people free through war is by saving their lives physically and delivering them from those who would kill them. We thank God for those who were rescued from the World Trade Center. We thank God for all those during World War II in the Pacific and in Europe who were set free from the terror of the Japanese and the Nazis. Do you remember the motion pictures of the U.S. troops marching through the various towns in France while the people lined the streets praising, thanking, hugging, and kissing them? And why? Because their lives were saved from Nazi terror and murder! It took American blood and the blood of other nations committed to resisting evil and fighting a just war to make this happen. War keeps people alive! War takes life; and war gives life. That's important to know.

We are fighting this war against Islamic terror to keep our kids and our grandkids alive! We are fighting this war to keep future generations alive. We are fighting this war to keep our nation and its values alive. God is at work in the war on terror—people will be set free. Their physical lives will be saved. Perhaps the lives of people in the Sudan who have been enslaved by Islamic fundamentalism will be delivered. Perhaps the Kurds in Saddam Hussein's Iraq will be set free from his terror and brutal subjugation. Perhaps those in Israel who are under attack daily by a variety of Islamic terror groups will for the first time find lasting freedom and security. And we could go on and on. Perhaps those in Afghanistan who now live under the brutal regime of the evil Taliban will find physical freedom and life again.

But God doesn't use war to just save physical life. In the very last verse of Esther chapter 8, we read this, "And many people of other nationalities became Jews because fear of the Jews had seized them." This means that God brought many of the Persians living in the 5th century BC to a true and saving knowledge of the God of Israel—the God of Abraham, Isaac and Jacob. And God did this in ancient Iran at the time when Zoroastrianism was beginning to take root and grow. God intervened in a war so that the Persian people could find spiritual freedom in God their Creator and Redeemer, the God revealed in the Old Testament scriptures. I believe God will bring many people to spiritual salvation through the gospel in the midst of the war on terror also.

I remember during the Persian Gulf War, when I was pastoring in Canada at the Metropolitan Bible Church in Ottawa, I did a sermon series on the whole issue of the gospel, prophecy, and the Middle East. We had a number of people come to Christ because God delights during wartime to get people focused on eternity and to bring them to a saving knowledge of and relationship with himself.

My barber is from Iran and I made sure I went to get a haircut this week. I wanted to assure him of the love and prayers of Christians for the people of Iran. I wanted to share again with him God's love for all people—Muslims, Jews, Christians, agnostics, atheists and everyone. He told me he escaped from the Ayatollah and the Islamic revolution many years ago. You should have heard this guy. He was saying, "Bomb all the terrorists! Start with Afghanistan, go after Iraq and then Iran—get them all. I lived under it and it is evil and it is wicked." I nodded as he spoke and realized that although the barbershop was full of people—it was eerily quiet. Normally there's a million conversations going on at once and you can barely hear yourself talk. But this particular day the only thing we were talking about was the horror of 9/11 and Islamic terrorism. Most of them knew I was a pastor and so they began to ask me—What do you think about all this? So I had a great opportunity to share the gospel with everybody in the barber shop.

I know that today is a divine appointment, and in the midst of this war on terror God wants you to know that he loves you, and he knows you by name. Jesus Christ died on that cross—in that tower—for you personally. He took your sins upon himself to set you free. Will you receive this free gift of salvation? Jesus Christ is the greatest gift God ever gave to the human race, and like every gift, you just need to receive it and say thank you. Don't turn your back on the grace of God!

GOD USES WAR TO FULFILL BIBLICAL PROPHECY

There is a third way that God uses war, and that is to fulfill biblical prophecy. We are living in the year 2001, a very short time in the history of the human race, a very short time in eternity. But long before history began, God ordained history. He ordained how it would begin, how he would intervene at the cross, and how he would consummate history and the kingdom—all in fulfillment of his prophecies in the Scriptures. And God will use this war against Islamic terror to fulfill prophecy as well. Let me give you an outstanding example of this.

Islamic terrorists hate both the Jews and Israel and want to destroy them and wipe them off the face of the earth. But God himself gave birth to the nation of Israel 3500 years ago under Moses—and orchestrated the rebirth of Israel in 1948. The Jews took possession of their land under the leadership of Joshua through the warfare described in the book of Joshua. God used the army of Israel to judge the Canaanite nations. But 1500 years later Jesus prophesied God's judgment on his own people as he looked out over the city of Jerusalem and wept saying:

> If you, even you, had only known on this day what would bring you peace—but now it is hidden from your eyes. The days will come upon you when your enemies will build an embankment against you and encircle you and hem you in on every side. They will dash you to the ground, you and the children within your

walls. They will not leave one stone on another, because you did not recognize the time of God's coming to you. (Luke 19:41-44)

God used the Roman-Jewish war to fulfill this prophecy. In AD 70, forty years after Jesus made the prophecy, the Roman General Titus, whose father was the Emperor Vespasian, attacked Jerusalem, killed tens of thousands of Jewish defenders, and destroyed the second temple—Herod's temple. And the Jewish people were flung throughout the world into a two thousand year dispersion—the Diaspora. Israel was born in war and Israel died in war. The birth of the nation and the death of the nation were all about war and prophecy. Once the Diaspora began in earnest, no one ever believed that the Jewish people and the nation of Israel would ever see the light of day again! But God had other plans.

The Old Testament prophets had proclaimed consistently that in the last days when the Messiah would come, the Jewish people would be in their homeland, and the nation would be established again. Ezekiel 36:24-28 says:

> For I will take you out of the nations; I will gather you from all the countries and bring you back into your own land. I will sprinkle clean water on you, and you will be clean; I will cleanse you from all your impurities and from all your idols. I will give you a new heart and put a new spirit in you; I will remove from you your heart of stone and give you a heart of flesh. And I will put my Spirit in you and move you to follow my decrees and be careful to keep my laws. Then you will live in the land I gave your ancestors; you will be my people, and I will be your God.

Ezekiel emphasizes that at the coming of the Messiah to establish his kingdom, the Jewish people will experience both a national and spiritual rebirth. That process began in 1948! The prophet Zechariah speaks of the Messiah's return to Jerusalem during a world war—the Battle of Armageddon—when God will physically deliver his people from an invasion of all the nations of the earth:

Then the LORD will go out and fight against those nations, as he fights on a day of battle. On that day his feet will stand on the Mount of Olives, east of Jerusalem, and the Mount of Olives will be split in two from east to west, forming a great valley, with half of the mountain moving north and half moving south. You will flee by my mountain valley, for it will extend to Azel. You will flee as you fled from the earthquake in the days of Uzziah king of Judah. Then the LORD my God will come, and all the holy ones with him. On that day there will be no light, no cold or frost. It will be a unique day, a day known only to the LORD—with no distinction between day and night. When evening comes, there will be light. On that day living water will flow out from Jerusalem, half of it east to the Dead Sea and half of it west to the Mediterranean Sea, in summer and in winter. The LORD will be king over the whole earth. On that day there will be one LORD, and his name the only name. (Zechariah 14:3-9)

God uses war to fulfill biblical prophecy. God did it in the Roman war and he did it in World War II, two thousand years later. Out of the ashes of the greatest conflict in human history, in which fifty million people were killed, including six million Jews in the Holocaust—God gave birth to the nation of Israel again, in fulfillment of biblical prophecy. Today in New York City, I wonder what prophecies God is fulfilling in the war on terror. You can be sure he is fulfilling some!

God Uses War To Demonstrate His Sovereignty

There is one final way that God uses war, and that is to demonstrate his sovereignty over nations and history. The Israeli-Palestinian conflict goes back thousands of years. One early example of this conflict was 3000 years ago when Israel faced off against the Philistines and David fought Goliath. 1 Samuel 17 describes this battle. The way they used to fight back then was very interesting—sometimes they would take the champion of one army and have him fight the champion of the other army. Two guys would fight and the guy who won—that army and that nation won the battle. Now that was real good if you had the toughest guy. In this case, it was the Philistines who had Goliath, this colossus of a man. I would compare him today to Osama Bin Laden, the world's most dangerous terrorist. In facing Islamic terrorism, we are facing a colossus. This is a very scary time. These people are evil, intelligent, well organized and full of hate. They have the potential to obtain and use weapons of mass destruction! We are facing Goliath today—without a doubt. And I want you to notice the impact of Goliath in verse 11, "...on hearing Goliath's words, Saul and all the Israelites were dismayed and terrified." Even strong men get scared. And that is why we as Americans must fight this war on two fronts—not just one. Our brave men and women are going to be fighting this war physically and militarily on what I call the eastern front. But even as Nazi Germany was eventually defeated because the war was finally fought on two fronts, so terrorism will be defeated because America will fight with courage and bravery militarily, but we will also fight spiritually, with faith, on the western front. As we trust God's Word, sacrifice, pray, show love and share the gospel—God will demonstrate his sovereignty as we wage war on both fronts.

David's victory over Goliath is both interesting and instructive. The Israelites were terrified, but David got impatient when he saw their fear. He asked in verse 26, "What's going to be done for the man who kills this Philistine and removes the disgrace from Israel? Who is this uncircumcised Philistine?" We might ask today, "Who are these wicked and evil terrorists killing innocent men, women and children?" The goal of Islamic terrorism is to instill fear, whether it's on a hijacked plane or in the barrenness of Afghanistan. Who is inflicting this terror on us? David said, "Who does he think he is defying the armies of the living God?" (vs. 26) And we say today in New York City as Christians, "Our God is alive! Our God is not some evil, wicked, malicious caricature of God. Our God is truly alive." The terrorists of 9/11 have made a mockery of the true God. In essence, David said that no one can stand before God when you mock him that way. David said to Saul in verses 34-37:

A Time *for* Hope

Your servant has been keeping his father's sheep. When a lion or a bear came and carried off a sheep from the flock, I went after it, struck it and rescued the sheep from its mouth. When it turned on me, I seized it by its hair, struck it and killed it. Your servant has killed both the lion and the bear; this uncircumcised Philistine will be like one of them, because he has defied the armies of the living God. The LORD who rescued me from the paw of the lion and the paw of the bear will rescue me from the hand of this Philistine.

And then David says to Goliath in verses 45-47:

You come against me with sword and spear and javelin, but I come against you in the name of the LORD Almighty, the God of the armies of Israel, whom you have defied. This day the LORD will deliver you into my hands, and I'll strike you down and cut off your head. This very day I will give the carcasses of the Philistine army to the birds and the wild animals, and the whole world will know that there is a God in Israel. All those gathered here will know that it is not by sword or spear that the LORD saves; for the battle is the LORD's, and he will give all of you into our hands.

David's God is alive, personal, mighty and sovereign. And so is ours!

So God uses war to demonstrate his sovereignty over nations and history. Our God is a sovereign God. President Bush has said that, "Freedom and fear, justice and cruelty, have long been at war and we know that God is not neutral between them." We are waging war on the western front spiritually. Ephesians 6 talks about the whole armor of God. Put on the truth. Be sincere. Let's not be hypocrites in this dark hour. Put on righteousness and holiness. We have been trying at Calvary Baptist Church in these last few days to be available to help and encourage people. We have people on site—doctors, pastors, counselors, police officers and volunteers to help. We have been keeping the church open to a constant stream of people who are afraid and need encouragement and want to pray with our pastors. We have set up a money fund which will be used to help hurting individuals and families. We are also receiving donations from people around the country who want to help New Yorkers in their time of need. We thank God that he brought the West Point Cadet Choir to encourage us here in New York City today!

We are blessed to have an amazing group of fire fighters right behind us on 58th Street. It is Engine Company 23—the Lion's Den! This company is full of New York's bravest who hosted our children during Vacation Bible School just two weeks before 9/11. They were wonderful to our kids, showing them the fire trucks and giving them a tour of the station house. Dr. Roy Roberts along with some of our education staff and our kids had the chance to do a short program for these wonderful men, sharing the good news of God's love with them. The theme for Vacation Bible School this summer was *Jesus to the Rescue*. Then, just a few days after this wonderful time together, many of these brave men gave their lives in the World Trade Center saving others. Jesus said, "Greater love has no man than this—than to give his life for his friends." (John 15:13) Our kids felt deeply the loss of these firemen and wanted to help their families. So the Sunday school collected $400 to bring back to the firehouse. When the firemen received these gifts from the children, a number of them came to the church to thank us with many tears and hugs. We will also use additional money being raised to immediately help the widows of these heroes. What a privilege.

We need faith today. This is part of the weapons of our warfare in Ephesians 6. I loved it when the President addressed Congress and the nation, and right above him it said, "In God we trust." In Christ we have assurance of our salvation. We are taught by the true God that we don't get to paradise by committing suicide in a terrorist act and by killing God's enemies. God never said you go to paradise by murdering people you believe are God's enemies. Jesus said on the cross to the thief who repented, "Today you shall be with me in paradise." (Luke 23:43) You don't go to paradise by killing God's enemies, you go to paradise by loving God's Son and trusting him and allowing him to help us to love God and our neighbor as ourselves.

The Bible is another weapon in our spiritual arsenal. God wants us to know his Word and to share it with love, but without compromise. We are to speak the truth in love. We are to be wise as serpents and innocent as doves. I received an interesting letter this week, right in the middle of all this suffering. This individual begins his letter saying:

> To the saints of Calvary Baptist Church in New York City—I am a pilot with American Airlines and I come to New York City occasionally. Every time I come, I come to Calvary. One time I brought a friend who is also a pilot to your church and as a result of that worship service he trusted Christ. Thank you for not being ashamed of the truth.

And this brother in Christ offered a generous gift to help in our relief efforts.

The final weapon of spiritual warfare mentioned in Ephesians 6 is prayer. We have had this church opened constantly for prayer in response to 9/11. So many people have come to pray. We have had Jews come in here and pray. We have had Catholics come in to this Baptist church and pray. We have had people from everywhere come in and pray. I had a New York City police officer come in a couple of days ago while I was on prayer duty with one of our associate pastors. This man, one of New York's finest, walked down the aisle and knelt at the prayer altar and spent some time in prayer. When he finished praying, I wanted to shake his hand and thank him. As I shook his hand he grabbed me in the biggest bear hug I think I have ever had and just about squeezed the life out of me. He said, "Thank you. Thank you for praying, thank you for being here." What a moment it was.

There were many American heroes who died on the flight that crashed in Pennsylvania. Heroes, who decided to resist the terrorists and take them down! One of those heroes was Todd Beamer, a New Jersey businessman, who was also a Sunday school teacher. He called out to his fellow passengers, as they began to try and take the plane back from the terrorists, "Help me, God! Help me, Jesus! Are you guys ready—let's roll!" That's when they attacked the terrorists. A telephone operator, who Todd spoke with from the airplane, heard his words on the phone before the plane crashed. Todd had given her detailed information about what was happening on the Newark to San Francisco flight. He then asked her to pray with him. Together they prayed the Lord's Prayer. The operator promised to call Todd's wife, which she did on Friday, after investigators gave her permission.

Their battle cry is our battle cry as well, as we fight spiritually for Christ and for his kingdom, "Help me, God! Help me, Jesus! Are you guys ready? Let's roll!" Like our President has prayed, "May God grant us wisdom, and may God watch over us, the United States of America."

In the name of God the Father and God the Son and God the Holy Spirit. Amen.

CHAPTER 3
A Time to Heal

In the days after 9/11, New Yorkers and Americans needed many things—we needed hope, which ultimately is found in God himself; we needed justice, which will be achieved by prosecuting a just war against Islamic terror; and we needed healing, which will take time because of the profound trauma to our hearts and minds. At Calvary Baptist Church, like many other places of worship, we had lost loved ones in the towers and seen others miraculously delivered.

One of the amazing escapes was Sam Jimenez Jr., who is the son of our deacon chairman. He was on the 87th floor of the north tower, just two floors below where the plane hit, and managed to get out safely. This is Sam's story:

> I had just come to work when we heard a huge explosion above us. We didn't know it then but a highjacked plane had struck the 89th floor of the north tower –two floors above us. The smoke was so bad we couldn't see, but somehow we made it to the stairway. A co-worker had unexpectedly brought 3 gallons of water to work that day—no one really knew why. We took off our shirts, drenched them in the water and used them to cover our faces in the suffocating smoke. I took a fire extinguisher from the 87th floor and carried it all the way to the

bottom, just in case we needed to break something open or put a fire out. When we got to the 14th floor, something inside of me said, "Run!" So I grabbed my co-worker and said, "We need to run faster!"

When we got to the ground floor, the lobby was in chaos because of all the panic and debris, so we were directed below the lobby to a safer exit on the other side of the building. We ended up by a support beam right next to the exit we were directed to—just then the south tower began to collapse. There was a great roar and our building trembled and shook like an earthquake. The force of the wind literally blew people and debris right by us. I was able to wrap my arms around the support beam and my coworker held on to me, and a pregnant lady grabbed and held on to my legs—and we all made it! During that tremendous roar I began to pray, "God please forgive me. Please have your angels protect me. Please don't let anything fall on me. Please get me through this." Then there was dead silence… and the smoke began to rise. My female co-worker had lost her sandals and there was broken glass everywhere—so I picked her up and carried her out of the building and then we saw the devastation outside.

The only injury I suffered was a small cut on my left hand, and ten years later there is just a little scar. It's there to remind me of the grace of God. The one thing that really struck me through this entire ordeal was that God was with me the whole time.

Sam Jr. then walked a few miles north to our church, joining others who were in shock, covered with dust and soot, looking like refugees. When he reached the church, we embraced and there were tears of joy and we thanked God for his amazing grace. We were then able to provide Sam and many others some practical help—changes of clothes, showers, transportation, money and phone calls to loved ones. Sam Jr. made a serious dedication of his life to God which continues today as he and his wife,

Judith, celebrate the birth of their daughter, Sarah, and Sam Sr. and Millie enjoy their first grandchild!

Another amazing escape was one of our church elders, Billy Boyd, who is an incredible professional chef and was working the morning of 9/11 on the 57th floor of the north tower when the plane struck. Billy's wife, Cathy, gives us her account of that terrible day:

> The morning of September 11, 2001 began as a routine busy day for me...but it's the one day, even though it was almost ten years ago, that I could still talk about like it happened just yesterday.
>
> As I was driving back home after taking my boys to school, I turned on the car radio, and the DJ was talking to somebody on the phone saying, "Can you please check this out for me, I heard that the top of the World Trade Center is on fire. I would appreciate any feedback on that..." I thought to myself, hmmm, the top of the WTC is on fire... its ok, Billy is on the 57th floor, that's halfway down. I parked the car, went into the apartment and turned the TV on. It was all over the news—the picture of one of the towers on fire and it wasn't on top as the guy on the radio had said. From an aerial view the fire was in the middle of one of the buildings. I picked up the phone and called his job. Every morning, Billy leaves the house at 4:30 a.m. to catch the 4:50 a.m. train to the city to get to work at 6:00 a.m. They had to set up for breakfast and lunch for corporate dining. Three weeks ago before 9/11, he was working in another building a few blocks away from the towers but got transferred to the account on the 57th floor of the north tower because their chef left. He had only been working there for three weeks. I remember him saying, "I can't wait to bring you guys up here one day, the view is incredible, it's breathtaking." We didn't have cell phones at that time, so I tried to call his boss from his previous account but I didn't get through. I left a message for

Billy to call me back...then suddenly the TV went blank. We didn't have cable, so I went to the next door neighbor and asked if I could watch the news with her. I told her that Billy was in the building and she started to panic and invited me in. Frantically, she asked me what I wanted her to do. She even asked me if I wanted her to call the mayor or something. I said, "It's ok, let's just wait." She said, "What are you talking about? Your husband is in there and you don't even know if he's OK or not!" She didn't understand why I was calm and just wanted to wait and at that point, I didn't understand why I wasn't in tears either. Another neighbor from the 4th floor came down to take my 2-year-old daughter Hannah and she was crying and very upset saying, "Let me have Hannah right now, and do what you need to do. I don't want you to become a widow." She took my daughter while I sat in front of the TV and watched and waited to hear from Billy. Suddenly right in front of our very eyes, one of the towers went down. My neighbor was going crazy over the whole thing! Between the tower falling and seeing me not doing anything made her even more frantic. When that building fell and I had not heard from Billy, I whispered a quiet prayer to the Lord, "Father, if Billy is in that building, he is in your hands. I know that he is safe in Your hands." I had received some calls from friends who didn't know that Billy was in the building, so I asked them to pray — and they did.

It wasn't until around 11:30 a.m. when my phone rang, and the gentleman on the other end said, "May I speak to Mrs. Boyd please." I said, "This is Mrs. Boyd, sir." He introduced himself as one of the corporate bosses calling from Pennsylvania, and he said that he wanted to let me know that Billy was able to get out of the building and is alright! I said, "Thank you sir." I hung up the phone and said to my neighbor, "Billy is alive" — and that's when I began to cry. I heard from Billy around 1:30 that afternoon telling me that he was OK and would try to get home soon.

Looking back a few days later, as I thought about how and why I was the way I was during the whole thing, I realized that God had prepared me for what was going to happen the next day. The night before I was doing my devotions and I was reading Psalm 57 verses 1 and 2 that said, "Have mercy on me, O God, have mercy on me. For in you my soul takes refuge. I will take refuge in the shadow of your wings until the disaster has passed. I cry out to God Most High, to God who fulfills his purpose for me." During the whole time, I knew God had his wings spread out covering Billy and me on each end. When I whispered that prayer, I entrusted him into God's hands knowing that if indeed God was going to take Billy home, I knew that he was safe in his hands and that the kids and I would also be safe because he will take care of us, too. God had another plan—keeping Billy safe and enabling him to get out of the building and to be with us today. This was God's way of fulfilling his promise in Jeremiah 29:11 "For I know the plans I have for you, declares the Lord, plans to prosper you and not to harm you, plans to give you hope and a future."

It took Billy 45 minutes to walk down all those stairs. He had offered to help the firefighters carry their equipment, but they thanked him and told him they wanted him to get safely out of the building. When Billy got out of the World Trade Center he went next door to his company's main office, and as they were looking out the window the first tower fell. No one seemed to know where to go after the building fell, so Billy said to his coworkers, "I'm going to Calvary—you can follow me if you want." And, of course, Calvary Baptist Church is on 57th Street in New York City. Billy had been on the 57th floor of the World Trade Center, and he escaped the towers and came to Calvary Baptist Church on 57th Street, and God gave Cathy Psalm 57 to meet her need in the midst of this tragedy. God really does work in mysterious ways!

Billy's message is:

> Be ready. It doesn't stop at inviting Christ into your life; it's
> about keeping Christ in your life. If you call out, he will answer.
> He will comfort. Those who made it out, who were spared or
> guided away, we were not given *a second chance at life*. It's
> not like a cat with nine lives. We get one chance. We get one
> life. Now we go forward with it.

Billy and Cathy had invested wisely in their relationship with God,
so when the calamity hit them head on, they were able to stand firm and
have a peace that even they could not understand. They impacted others
spiritually in the crisis because they had been impacted by God through
his Word. Billy and Cathy were an amazing testimony to their neighbors
and co-workers in the midst of the suffering, chaos and tragedy.

So as I prepared to preach to my people on the third Sunday after 9/11,
I had healing on my mind…

Sunday, September 30, 2001

We have been seeking hope together these last few weeks, which is
God's gift through the cross of Jesus Christ; and we have been seeking
justice, which will be achieved in the war on terror; but God is also Jeho-
vah Rapha, the God who heals us—and he will touch and restore our
hearts and our minds and our spirit.

God knows the territory of suffering. He knows how to navigate the
fog of pain and loss. He tells us quietly that he has *been there—done that*.
He is Immanuel—*God with us*. And he is healing us even as he has been
healing many of the survivors and families brutalized by the terror of Columbine 2 ½ years ago.

One of the precious young people murdered at Columbine High School
was Rachel Scott. Her father, Darrell, has been sharing her story to help
bring hope and healing to those bereaved by the terror of 9/11. He shares
a powerful testimony about his daughter, Rachel, in a pamphlet published

by the Kings College and Priority Associates. The title of the pamphlet is *remembrance, September 11, 2001—fallen but not forgotten* and Mr. Scott's moving contribution is called "Honor Their Memory—Do Not Let Them Die in Vain" (page 6-7). It is important that you hear Darrell Scott this morning as we seek healing also:

> One moment you are just going through the routine of another day, and the next moment your life is shattered. I know the feeling well, because it happened to me on April 20, 1999.

> My daughter, Rachel Scott, was brutally gunned down while sitting on the grass eating her lunch at Columbine High School. She was a beautiful, talented, energetic, and optimistic teenager with so much to live for. And in one moment's time, she was no longer there...

After sharing his love for his daughter and his immense grief and pain over her loss, he honors her with a moving poem and tribute. His final words concern the hope for healing:

> I know the transforming power of a loving God who can create the universe out of nothing, and can take the worst of tragedies and bring purpose, life and meaning from it. Whether the location is a high school, skyscraper, military complex, airplane cabin, or a hill called Calvary, tragedy can be turned into triumph...

> I am so grateful that I chose to turn to my heavenly Father for strength and comfort in my personal loss. There I found the courage to forgive, the strength to let go and the ability to see beyond the tragedy to a divine purpose that has slowly emerged with time.

> We all have the ability to make choices. Those choices may leave us either bitter or better. Those choices include honoring our departed loved ones and their memories. You are now a continuation of the lives of those you have lost. Make them proud.

A TIME *for* HOPE

Only God can give genuine healing—healing that empowers us and transform us. But we have a role to play. For America to be healed, God's people must play a leading role—we have a very special privilege and responsibility in the healing process. For America to be healed the church must humble itself before God! But how? The need is great, and hearts are so hurt, damaged and brutalized—and then the Lord shows us how.

The story of the dedication of Solomon's Temple nearly 3,000 years ago, and Solomon's prayer of dedication, recorded in 2 Chronicles 6-7, is instructive for us today as we respond to the horror of 9/11. God knew that his people were at times going to rebel against him, and that he would need to bring judgment upon them. So what was to be the response of God's people to God's judgment upon them? God says to Solomon in 2 Chronicle 7:12-14:

> I have heard your prayer and have chosen this place for myself as a temple for sacrifices. When I shut up the heavens so that there is no rain, or command locusts to devour the land or send a plague among my people—if my people, who are called by my name, will humble themselves and pray and seek my face and turn from their wicked ways, then I will hear from heaven, and I will forgive their sin and will heal their land.

What an awesome God—and what an awesome responsibility we have before God!

IF MY PEOPLE...WILL HUMBLE THEMSELVES

Notice God's emphasis in the midst of a divine judgment and the need for national repentance: "If **MY people**, called by **MY name** will **humble themselves**..." God says national healing and restoration always begins with the humble response of the people of God! It doesn't start with unbelievers and pagans and skeptics (who are loved by God, even though they don't know it)—it starts with people who know they are loved by God. It starts with us.

To say that the church doesn't always understand this is an understatement of the tenth magnitude! In the aftermath of the loss and suffering of 9/11, in the heat and passion and grief of the moment, there were a few statements made by some prominent evangelical leaders, including Jerry Falwell, which were irresponsible, hateful and dishonoring to God. I love Jerry Falwell as a brother in Christ, and I have great respect for much of his ministry and testimony. I also agree with him on the major doctrines of our faith, and I have had the privilege of meeting him on two occasions during the course of my ministry. But there are times when I have had to stand in this pulpit and repudiate certain things that he and other evangelical leaders have said, because we are also an evangelical Baptist church—and we don't want to be painted with the same brush as we try to love and reach New York City for Christ.

In blaming these attacks on homosexuals, abortionists, feminists, the ACLU and others, Rev. Falwell was blind to the truth that "judgment begins in the house of God." (1 Peter 4:17) It's always about us. I take serious issue with both the misplaced emphasis and the unloving tone of his remarks. It is a misplaced emphasis because God judges his people first—he judges *our* self-righteousness, greed, selfishness, arrogance, and neglect of love, justice and compassion. And an unloving tone is always unacceptable to God who commands us "to speak the truth in love." (Ephesians 4:15)

I encourage my brother Rev. Falwell to keep the promise he made publicly to the evangelical church and the American people a few years ago after the PTL fiasco—that he would quit playing politics and get back to preaching the gospel. I also encourage him, if these are the kind of statements he is going to continue to make, to please stay off the television for awhile—because your public comments are hurting the cause of Christ big time in this city and in this nation right now. (NOTE: Not long after this message was preached, Rev. Falwell publicly repented and asked forgiveness for his unloving comments. To his credit, he was willing to take responsibility for his actions, and I commend him for this. This is, sadly, more than we can say for some other evangelical leaders who have dishonored the Lord with false and unloving statements concerning the causes of 9/11, and have never taken responsibility).

The parable Jesus told in Luke 18:9-14 is instructive for all of us who desire to follow Jesus Christ in a loving and credible manner:

> To some who were confident of their own righteousness and looked down on everyone else, Jesus told this parable: Two men went up to the temple to pray, one a Pharisee and the other a tax collector. The Pharisee stood by himself and prayed: "God, I thank you that I am not like other people—robbers, evildoers, adulterers—or even like this tax collector. I fast twice a week and give a tenth of all I get." But the tax collector stood at a distance. He would not even look up to heaven, but beat his breast and said, "God, have mercy on me, a sinner." I tell you that this man, rather than the other, went home justified before God. For all those who exalt themselves will be humbled, and those who humble themselves will be exalted.

Of course, everyone in America must humble themselves before God—as Paul said to the Athenians in Acts 17:30, "But now God commands all people everywhere to repent." America must stop worshipping and trusting our national idols of economic power, military power, political power and cultural power—and it is God's people who must lead the way by rejecting our own idols! James chastises and challenges the church in James 4:1-10:

> What causes fights and quarrels among you? Don't they come from your desires that battle within you? You desire but do not have, so you kill. You covet but you cannot get what you want, so you quarrel and fight. You do not have because you do not ask God. When you ask, you do not receive, because you ask with wrong motives, that you may spend what you get on your pleasures. You adulterous people, don't you know that friendship

with the world means enmity against God? Therefore, anyone who chooses to be a friend of the world becomes an enemy of God. Or do you think Scripture says without reason that he jealously longs for the spirit he has caused to dwell in us? But he gives us more grace. That is why Scripture says: God opposes the proud but shows favor to the humble. Submit yourselves, then, to God. Resist the devil, and he will flee from you. Come near to God and he will come near to you. Wash your hands, you sinners, and purify your hearts, you double-minded. Grieve, mourn and wail. Change your laughter to mourning and your joy to gloom. Humble yourselves before the Lord, and he will lift you up.

IF MY PEOPLE...WILL PRAY

The second thing God's people must do is pray. "If *my people*, called by *my name*, will humble themselves and *pray*..." (2 Chronicles 7:14) The connection between prayer and personal and national healing and renewal is a powerful one. We have seen this throughout history with the revivals that have attended prayer movements resulting in the first and second Great Awakenings. New York City experienced this in the Fulton Street Revival—God's people humbling themselves and praying for their leaders, their city and their nation. James reveals the connection between prayer and healing in the context of persecution and spiritual warfare when he writes in James 5:13-18:

> Is anyone among you in trouble? Let them pray. Is anyone happy? Let them sing songs of praise. Is anyone among you sick? Let them call the elders of the church to pray over them and anoint them with oil in the name of the Lord. And the prayer offered in faith will make the sick person well; the Lord will raise them up. If they have sinned, they will be forgiven. Therefore confess your sins to each other and pray for each other so that you may be healed. The prayer of a righteous person is powerful and effective. Elijah was a human being, even as we are. He prayed ear-

nestly that it would not rain, and it did not rain on the land for three and a half years. Again he prayed, and the heavens gave rain, and the earth produced its crops.

The terrorists are praying! They are praying to their God of hate and murder after ceremoniously cleansing themselves in the ultimate act of spiritual hypocrisy! Clean yourself up and pray and then go slaughter innocent men, women and children—all for your God! They are probably praying more than we are!

Mohammad Atta was one of the leaders of this evil 9/11 attack. He said to his fellow terrorists: "We need to utilize those few hours that are left to ask God for forgiveness." They prayed for forgiveness ahead of time, knowing that murder is evil! What God encourages such a perverse prayer? Not the God who created the universe and sent Christ to be the Savior of the world. Atta also exhorted his Muslim brothers, "Make sure nobody follows you. Make sure that you are clean—your clothes are clean and your shoes." He told them to make sure everything is clean on the outside, even though everything is filthy and ugly and vicious on the inside! "In the morning," he said, "try to pray the morning prayer with an open heart. Don't leave until you have washed for prayer. Continue to pray when you enter the plane 'Oh God, open all doors for me'." What an abomination—what hypocrisy—what wickedness! May the one true God judge this evil even as we trust him to turn the hearts of terrorists to Christ. Terrorists are praying! In Afghanistan they pray while they enslave Christian women who are there to help the poor and to share the love of Christ. They pray as they pump bullets into the heads of Muslim women who have offended them and their God. They execute them in the public square in cold blood—as they offer their prayers.

As Christians we have a relationship with the one true God—the God of love and power. The question is: Are we praying?

I was struck by the service at Yankee Stadium, as I watched on television Sunday afternoon in between my services at Calvary. The service was held to bring the community together to pray and to celebrate as Americans our shared values of faith and freedom. My favorite moment was the singing of the Battle Hymn of the Republic. I wasn't sure if they would sing the third stanza because of the ecumenical nature of the service, but thank God they did: "In the beauty of the lilies, Christ was born across the sea, with a glory in his bosom that transfigures you and me: As he died to make men holy, let us die to make men free, while God is marching on. Glory, glory hallelujah...."

Humble prayer before the true God is powerful. Solomon, in the time he actually walked with God, was a man of prayer. At the dedication of the temple in Jerusalem, almost 3,000 years ago, the Bible says:

> Then Solomon stood before the altar of the LORD in front of the whole assembly of Israel and spread out his hands. Now he had made a bronze platform, five cubits long, five cubits wide and three cubits high, and had placed it in the center of the outer court. He stood on the platform and then knelt down before the whole assembly of Israel and spread out his hands toward heaven. He said: "LORD, the God of Israel, there is no God like you in heaven or on earth—you who keep your covenant of love with your servants who continue wholeheartedly in your way. You have kept your promise to your servant David my father; with your mouth you have promised and with your hand you have fulfilled it—as it is today. Now, LORD, the God of Israel, keep for your servant David my father the promises you made to him when you said, "You shall never fail to have a successor to sit before me on the throne of Israel, if only your descendants are careful in all they do to walk before me according to my law, as you have done." And now, LORD, the God of Israel, let your word that you promised your servant David come true." (2 Chronicles 6:12-17)

And then Solomon ended his prayer with a powerful appeal, and God responded in an even more spectacular way:

> Now, my God, may your eyes be open and your ears attentive to the prayers offered in this place. Now arise, LORD God,

and come to your resting place, you and the ark of your might. May your priests, LORD God, be clothed with salvation, may your faithful people rejoice in your goodness. LORD God, do not reject your anointed one. Remember the great love promised to David your servant. When Solomon finished praying, fire came down from heaven and consumed the burnt offering and the sacrifices, and the glory of the LORD filled the temple. The priests could not enter the temple of the LORD because the glory of the LORD filled it. When all the Israelites saw the fire coming down and the glory of the LORD above the temple, they knelt on the pavement with their faces to the ground, and they worshiped and gave thanks to the LORD, saying, "He is good; his love endures forever." (2 Chronicles 6:40- 7:3)

God wants his people and his leaders to humble themselves and pray. Solomon's example certainly influenced King Jehoshaphat years later when he was confronted by a major terror threat from the Moabites and Ammonites—and his first response was humble prayer:

Alarmed, Jehoshaphat resolved to inquire of the LORD, and he proclaimed a fast for all Judah. The people of Judah came together to seek help from the LORD; indeed, they came from every town in Judah to seek him. Then Jehoshaphat stood up in the assembly of Judah and Jerusalem at the temple of the LORD in the front of the new courtyard and said: "LORD, the God of our ancestors, are you not the God who is in heaven? You rule over all the kingdoms of the nations. Power and might are in your hand, and no one can withstand you. Our God, did you not drive out the inhabitants of this land before your people Israel and give it forever to the descendants of Abraham your friend?...Our God, will you not judge them? For we have no power to face this vast army that is attacking us. We do not know what to do, *but our eyes are on you.*" *All the men of Judah, with their wives and children and little ones, stood there before the LORD.* (2 Chronicles 20:5-13)

One of the sights that continues to grip me the most at Ground Zero is the brave rescue workers who work so hard and risk their own lives to retrieve the precious bodies of dead loved ones. And each time they find one, suddenly there is a prayer circle. And it's overwhelming—it touches us deeply—as these strong, brave New Yorkers bow their heads and pray together. We see rescue workers praying over victims, people praying for their missing family and friends, churches and young people, including our own youth group at Calvary, having prayer walks and praying over the posters of missing people. How awesome is our God and the healing power he gives us through prayer.

The question for us today is: Am I praying? Are you praying? Are we at Calvary Baptist Church praying? We have a prayer meeting this Wednesday night at 7 p.m.—it's always been there. We have a half night of prayer this Friday at Calvary from 6 p.m. to 10 p.m. We have had it there for three years. We had a special prayer meeting this past Thursday night with Joni Eareckson Tada. We have had special times of prayer during this tragedy—but thank God for the regular times of prayer we have. May the Lord convict us. May the Lord lead us to be praying people.

IF MY PEOPLE...WILL SEEK MY FACE

When we humble ourselves and pray—we are seeking God! "If *my people*, who are called by *my name*, will humble themselves and pray and *seek my face*..." (2 Chronicles 7:14).

Joni Eareckson-Tada was here Thursday night and she gave a wonderful testimony of God's love and grace in the midst of such suffering. It reminded me very much of Job. She talked about the fact that when she was a teenager and lived in Maryland—not far from where I grew up and only a one-year difference in our ages—she broke her neck and severed her spine in a diving accident. As a young girl she learned to trust God in the midst of her agony. She was angry at God. She questioned God. And God in his love gave her room and space to be herself and to express herself. God eventually began to heal her mind and heart and began to show her that he is a great and sovereign God. God taught her that he redeems suffering for the purpose of glorifying his name and bringing his children into a closer relationship with himself.

Joni's story reminds me of Job. He lost his children, he lost his health, he lost his livelihood and he almost lost his marriage. Yet in the midst of all this unspeakable suffering, Job continued to seek and to worship God:

> At this, Job got up and tore his robe and shaved his head. Then he fell to the ground in worship and said: "Naked I came from my mother's womb, and naked I will depart. The LORD gave and the LORD has taken away; may the name of the LORD be praised." In all this, Job did not sin by charging God with wrongdoing. (Job 1:20-22)

Eventually, however, the horrendous suffering, inner turmoil and conflict brought Job to despair—and he poured out his anguished heart:

> After this, Job opened his mouth and cursed the day of his birth. He said: "May the day of my birth perish, and the night that said, 'A boy is conceived!' That day—may it turn to darkness; may God above not care about it; may no light shine on it. May gloom and utter darkness claim it once more; may a cloud settle over it; may blackness overwhelm it. That night—may thick darkness seize it; may it not be included among the days of the year nor be entered in any of the months. May that night be barren; may no shout of joy be heard in it. May those who curse days curse that day, those who are ready to rouse Leviathan. May its morning stars become dark; may it wait for daylight in vain and not see the first rays of dawn, for it did not shut the doors of the womb on me to hide trouble from my eyes." (Job 3:1-10)

Job literally stopped wanting to live anymore. He couldn't bear to welcome another sunrise. But God had a purpose—he was bringing Job into a deeper relationship with himself:

> Then Job replied to the LORD: "I know that you can do all things; no purpose of yours can be thwarted." You asked, "Who

is this that obscures my plans without knowledge?" Surely I spoke of things I did not understand, things too wonderful for me to know." You said, "Listen now, and I will speak; I will question you, and you shall answer me. *My ears had heard of you but now my eyes have seen you.* Therefore I despise myself and repent in dust and ashes." (Job 42:1-6)

It was then that God poured out his blessing and his healing:

The LORD blessed the latter part of Job's life more than the former part. He had fourteen thousand sheep, six thousand camels, a thousand yoke of oxen and a thousand donkeys. And he also had seven sons and three daughters. The first daughter he named Jemimah, the second Keziah and the third Keren-Happuch. Nowhere in all the land were there found women as beautiful as Job's daughters, and their father granted them an inheritance along with their brothers. After this, Job lived a hundred and forty years; he saw his children and their children to the fourth generation. And so Job died, an old man and full of years. (Job 42:12-17)

IF MY PEOPLE...WILL TURN FROM THEIR WICKED WAYS

For the healing to begin in New York City and America, the church, just like Job, must be the first to repent and turn from our own wickedness! "If *my people*, who are called by *my name*, will humble themselves and pray and seek my face and *turn from their wicked ways*..." (2 Chronicles 7:14)

Daniel knew the need for personal and national repentance in the face of God's judgment on Israel and her deportation to Babylon. In Daniel 9:1-9,19 we hear Daniel's repentance for himself and for his people:

In the first year of Darius son of Xerxes (a Mede by descent), who was made ruler over the Babylonian kingdom— in the first year of his reign, I, Daniel, understood from the Scriptures, according to the word of the LORD given to Jeremiah the prophet, that the desolation of Jerusalem would last seventy years. So I turned to the Lord God and pleaded with him in prayer and petition, in fasting, and in sackcloth and ashes. I prayed to the LORD my God and confessed: "Lord, the great and awesome God, who keeps his covenant of love with those who love him and keep his commandments, we have sinned and done wrong. We have been wicked and have rebelled; we have turned away from your commands and laws. We have not listened to your servants the prophets, who spoke in your name to our kings, our princes and our ancestors, and to all the people of the land. Lord, you are righteous, but this day we are covered with shame—the people of Judah and the inhabitants of Jerusalem and all Israel, both near and far, in all the countries where you have scattered us because of our unfaithfulness to you. We and our kings, our princes and our ancestors are covered with shame, LORD, because we have sinned against you. The Lord our God is merciful and forgiving, even though we have rebelled against him...Lord, listen! Lord, forgive! Lord, hear and act! For your sake, my God, do not delay, because your city and your people bear your Name."

It is vitally important for the church, even as we support a just war against Islamic terrorism to constantly look at our own hearts and lives, so that we can be a source of renewal and healing in our nation, and not a cause of future divine judgment!

In Luke 13:1-5, Jesus tells an amazing story that could have come right out of the headlines of the Jerusalem Post 2000 years ago or the New York Times today. He said:

Now there were some present at that time who told Jesus about the Galileans whose blood Pilate had mixed with their sacrifices.

Pontius Pilate was persecuting the Jews at that time and had executed people and mingled their blood with the temple sacrifices that were being offered to God. And Jesus said to the people:

> Do you think that these Galileans were worse sinners than all
> the other Galileans because they suffered this way?

I am sure a lot of people at that time would have said: Oh yes, Lord. I'm sure they are worse because we see the judgment. Jesus is saying don't be so quick to see the judgment of God on other people. He says:

> I tell you, no! But unless **you** repent, **you,** too, will all perish.

He doesn't just mean physical death but eternal death as well. And then Jesus asks them:

> What about those eighteen people who died when the tower in
> Siloam fell on them—do you think they were more guilty than
> all the others living in Jerusalem? I tell you, no! But unless **you**
> repent, **you** too will all perish.

Jesus asks us today—what about those thousands of precious people from almost 100 nations who died on 9/11 when the towers fell on them? Do you think they were more wicked and sinful people than you and I who still take breath today? And some of us are quick to say—Oh they must have been. And Jesus is even quicker to say—Oh no, not at all. God loves them also. He offers everyone love, grace and forgiveness. Then Jesus says, "But I tell *you* unless *you* repent, *you* too will perish."

I urge you today, if you are here without Christ, don't take second chances for granted. Our life is a vapor—it's precious to God; but, it's here and it's gone. Receive Jesus Christ today, in the quiet of your own heart, ask him to forgive you, to set you free, to give you a new life, to make you a child of God. Tell him that you want to follow him now as the Lord of your life.

And as believers, we need to make a new commitment as God's people, called by God's name, in his power to humble ourselves daily, to pray daily, to seek his face daily, and to repent of our wickedness moment by moment, that he might use us as an instrument of healing for our great city and nation. The Lord says that repentance begins with *my* people who are called by *my* name!

GOD'S GRACIOUS RESPONSE

Notice God's response to his people's repentance: "If ***my people***, who are called by ***my name***, will humble themselves and pray, and seek my face, and turn from their wicked ways ***then I will hear from heaven and forgive their sin and heal their land.***" (2 Chronicles 7:14) When God's people repent:

- ✦ God hears us.
- ✦ God forgives us.
- ✦ God heals us.

There is no suffering that God cannot redeem; there is no heart that God cannot heal; there is no nation that God cannot restore.

It is hard to imagine any suffering greater than that of the patriarch Joseph, who was sold into slavery by his own brothers—after they threatened to kill him! He was brutalized and betrayed by his own flesh and blood! And in Egypt, in a strange land without family, without friends, and apparently without hope—the Bible assures us that "the Lord was with Joseph." (Genesis 39:21-23) And God used Joseph mightily and blessed him and gave him certain promises which strengthened and sustained him:

- ✦ I will be with you in the wilderness.
- ✦ I will use you in the wilderness.
- ✦ I will heal you in the wilderness.

And God ***was with*** Joseph, and ***used*** him, and ***healed*** him! In Genesis 41:50-52 we read of God's blessing and healing:

Before the years of famine came, two sons were born to Joseph by Asenath daughter of Potiphera, priest of On. Joseph named

his firstborn Manasseh and said, "It is because God has made
me forget all my trouble and all my father's household." The
second son he named Ephraim and said, "It is because God has
made me fruitful in the land of my suffering."

God healed Joseph's mind and his heart—and redeemed his suffering.
And God gave Joseph an understanding of how God uses everything for
good—even the bad and ugly things—God never wastes the suffering!

After many years, Joseph encountered his brothers and revealed his
identity to them. Can you imagine their shock and shame when they first
saw him! And then we see the profound effect of Joseph's growing understanding of suffering:

Then Joseph said to his brothers, "Come close to me." When
they had done so, he said, "I am your brother Joseph, the one
you sold into Egypt! And now, do not be distressed and do not
be angry with yourselves for selling me here, because it was to
save lives that God sent me ahead of you. For two years now
there has been famine in the land, and for the next five years
there will be no plowing and reaping. But God sent me ahead
of you to preserve for you a remnant on earth and to save your
lives by a great deliverance. So then, *it was not you who sent
me here, but God*. He made me father to Pharaoh, lord of his
entire household and ruler of all Egypt." (Genesis 45:4-8)

Years later, at the death of their father, Jacob, Joseph's brothers were
concerned that Joseph would finally take his revenge on them:

When Joseph's brothers saw that their father was dead, they
said, "What if Joseph holds a grudge against us and pays us
back for all the wrongs we did to him?" So they sent word
to Joseph, saying, "Your father left these instructions before
he died: This is what you are to say to Joseph: I ask you to
forgive your brothers the sins and the wrongs they committed in treating you so badly. Now please forgive the sins of

the servants of the God of your father." When their message came to him, Joseph wept. His brothers then came and threw themselves down before him. "We are your slaves," they said. But Joseph said to them, "Don't be afraid. Am I in the place of God? *You intended to harm me, but God intended it for good to accomplish what is now being done*, the saving of many lives. So then, don't be afraid. I will provide for you and your children." And he reassured them and spoke kindly to them. (Genesis 50:15-21)

Joseph had been transformed by God through suffering—He had been healed and set free. This is God's promise to us as well—and to all who will trust him and serve him.

Billy Graham has been America's pastor for a long time—and he gets better with age! Many presidents have called upon him to bring a word of hope to the nation during times of national tragedy, and God has used him mightily. In the last few days, Rev. Graham spoke to the American people from the pulpit of the National Cathedral, and offered us hope for healing:

We've always needed God from the very beginning of this nation, but today we need him especially. The Bible's words are our hope: "God is our refuge and strength, an ever present help in trouble. Therefore we will not fear, though the earth give way and the mountains fall into the heart of the sea". (Psalm 46:1-2)

But why does God allow evil like this to take place? Perhaps that is what you are asking. You may even be angry at God. I want to assure you that God understands those feelings. And God can be trusted, even when life seems at its darkest."

I have been asked hundreds of times why God allows tragedy and suffering. I have to confess that I really do not know the answer totally, even to my own satisfaction. I have to accept, by faith, that God is sovereign and he is a God of love and mercy and compassion in the midst of suffering.

None of us will ever forget the pictures of our courageous fire-fighters and police or the hundreds standing patiently in line to donate blood. A tragedy like this could have torn this country apart, but instead it has united us and we have become a family.

We never know when we, too, will be called into eternity. I doubt if even one of those people who got on those planes, or walked into the World Trade Center or the Pentagon that morning thought it would be the last day of their lives. And that's why each of us needs to face our own spiritual need and commit ourselves to God and his will now.

Yes, our nation has been attacked, buildings destroyed and lives lost. But now we have a choice: whether to implode and disintegrate emotionally and spiritually as a people and a nation, or to rebuild on a solid foundation. I believe we are in the process of starting to rebuild. That foundation is our trust in God.

My prayer today is that we will feel the loving arms of God wrapped around us, and will know in our hearts that he will never forsake us as we trust in Him.

In the name of God the Father and God the Son and God the Holy Spirit. Amen.

CHAPTER 4
A Time for Peace

SUNDAY, OCTOBER 6, 2001

There is no doubt that on 9/11 evil paid us a terrible visit. There is also no doubt that the warfare and terrorism of the Middle East struck New York City and America on 9/11. Some of the same Islamic terror that strikes Israel on a regular basis, perpetrated by Hamas, Hezbollah and Islamic Jihad—we have now experienced from Al-Qaeda. It is true that Hamas has not been linked to the terror here—not yet—but Hamas has been linked to Al-Qaeda in the past. Hezbollah has not been linked to the 9/11 attacks yet, but Hezbollah has been directly linked to Bin Laden and Al-Qaeda in the bombings of the US Embassies in Kenya and Tanzania. You can be absolutely sure that we were struck by Middle East terror on 9/11!

Secretary of Defense Donald Rumsfeld has a very difficult task as he serves in the administration of President Bush, our Commander in Chief, along with the Joint Chiefs of Staff—who must now wage military war against Islamic terrorists. What a challenge! But I believe that the person who has an even more difficult challenge is Secretary of State Colin Powell. How would you like to have his job? In the midst of the war on terror, his task is to broker a peace treaty between Israel and the Palestinians. Colin Powell clearly has the greater task—without a doubt!

A TIME *for* HOPE

Who can mediate a Middle East peace? Who can broker peace? Who can bring peace to Middle Eastern hearts and minds—to Middle Eastern peoples, nations and religions? Whoever is going to accomplish such a monumental task is going to have to be much more than just a peace lover. It's easy to love peace—most of us do. We thank God for peace lovers— those who cherish peace and work tirelessly to achieve it. We thank God for those who sincerely from their hearts want to "give peace a chance." We want peace. We want to see world peace restored and established once and for all. But peace-loving is not peace-making! It takes far more than loving peace to actually make peace.

To make peace in the Middle East is also going to require more than *peacekeepers*. Peace-keeping is difficult, dangerous and necessary—it is a noble endeavor. But it's not the peacekeepers who become the peace-makers. Modern peace-keeping is usually defined as "the time it takes for enemies to reload." To establish peace in the Middle East and the world will include peace lovers and peacekeepers—but will ultimately require actual peacemakers.

The biblical Greek word for peace is *eirene*—from which we get the English word *irenic*. What a world it would be if everyone had an irenic spirit! It's going to take a peace-maker to bring *eirene* to Israeli and Pal-estinian hearts. A peacemaker is required to bring wholeness, well being, security and hope to the Middle East. This is the meaning of the Hebrew word for peace—*shalom*. It's going to take a peacemaker to establish active good will in the hearts of Yasser Arafat and Ariel Sharon and all the other major players on the Middle East stage today. A peacemaker actu-ally takes enemies and turns them into friends. A peacemaker is actually able to replace active malice and hostility with active good will—*shalom*! Now who is capable of this?

I have a world of respect for President Bush, Colin Powell and Donald Rumsfeld, and also for those who worked for peace before them—Presi-dent Clinton, Madeline Albright, Henry Kissinger and others—all of whom made a significant contribution in the search for peace. But they couldn't get it done! Why? Because as smart as they are—they aren't smart enough. And as powerful and influential as they are—even they don't have enough clout! They aren't tough enough! And as passionate as they are—they aren't passionate enough. They don't have enough love. There is only one man who can make peace in the Middle East, in the world and in human hearts—and his name is Jesus Christ.

America was targeted on 9/11—we were attacked—because we are hated by Islamic terrorists. It is important to understand just how much we are hated! They hate us because of our freedom, because of our Judeo-Christian faith tradition, and because of our friends—particularly our friendship with and support of Israel and the Jewish people. Recently Bin Laden himself went public with this message:

> The people of Islam have suffered from aggression, iniquity and injustice imposed by the Zionist crusader alliance and their collaborators. It is now the duty of every tribe in the Arabian Peninsula to fight jihad and to cleanse the land from these crusader occupiers. Their wealth is booty to those who kill them. My Muslim brothers, your brothers in Palestine and in the land of the two holy places (*Saudi Arabia*) are calling upon your help and asking you to take part in fighting against the enemy—the Americans and the Israelis. They are asking you to do whatever you can to expel the enemies out of the sanctuaries of Islam.

There is nothing like a message from a *man of god*! By Zionist crusaders, Bin Laden means the Jews and the Americans. Bin Laden hates the Jews and Americans with a passion. We are at war and according to Bin Laden we are public enemy number one.

There is one man—but only one—who can literally transform terrorists' hearts. There is only one person who can change our hearts, Israeli hearts and Palestinian hearts—only one! Whoever is going to achieve this miracle of peace is going to need a passion for peace—a passion like no other person who has ever lived. To find this person and passion we need to consider an event described in Luke 19, which highlights the passion required to bring peace to the Middle East and to the world. In

A TIME *for* HOPE

Luke 19:41 we read that, "As Jesus approached Jerusalem and saw the city, he *wept* over it..." It's going to take that kind of passion and love. We can hear Jesus crying out, 2000 years ago, to the Jewish people who had rejected him. We can hear him crying out today to the people of Jerusalem, the Middle East and the world—to Jews, Muslims, Christians, Hindus, Buddhists, atheists; to all people—calling out as he weeps over our world, "If you, even you, had only known on this day what would bring you peace—but now it is hidden from your eyes." (vs.42) Literally, a judicial blindness afflicted the Jewish people of Jesus' day—and continues to impact the human race today, Jew and Gentile alike. We are blind to the fact that there is only one Peacemaker and his name is Jesus Christ. Jesus went on to prophesy the judgment against his own people in verses 43-44:

> The days will come upon you when your enemies will build
> an embankment against you (*Jerusalem*) and encircle you and
> hem you in on every side. They will dash you to the ground,
> you and the children within your walls. They will not leave
> one stone on another, because you did not recognize the time of
> God's coming to you.

Jesus demonstrates a passion for peace and a love for people—but also a jealousy for the holiness and justice of God. Forty years after Jesus gave that prophecy, General Titus, the son of Emperor Vespasian of Rome, along with his Roman legions engaged the Jews in the Roman wars, defeated the Israeli army, destroyed the city of Jerusalem and burned the temple, the great second temple of Zerubbabel and Herod the Great. The Romans literally built embankments of wood scaffolding all around, using huge quantities of wood, and they set it all on fire. It was so hot in the inferno that the stones and marble and gold literally melted in the heat and were destroyed. But long before the judgment ever fell, you can listen to the heart of Jesus as he looked over the city of Jerusalem and wept over the people:

> Jerusalem, Jerusalem, you who kill the prophets and stone
> those sent to you, how often I have longed to gather your chil-

dren together, as a hen gathers her chicks under her wings, and you were not willing. Look, your house is left to you desolate. For I tell you, you will not see me again until you say, "Blessed is he who comes in the name of the Lord." (Matthew 23:37-39)

What Jesus was saying is if only you had known the one who can bring you peace, the one who truly loves you and wants to forgive you and make you free—but you did not recognize me. You did not receive me.

Passion for peace is good—but passion is not enough. It takes a special person with a special resumé to pull it off. There's got to be a resumé! And that person and that resumé were predicted by the prophet Isaiah 2700 years ago. In Isaiah 9, in a passage that we traditionally hear at Christmas, we read these words in verse 6, "For unto us a child is born, unto us a son is given..." This is usually presented as referring only to the birth of the Messiah (His first coming), but this context also includes the kingdom of the Messiah (His second coming). We must address both the first and second coming of the Messiah to get a clear and accurate picture of him. This child eventually grew up to be the man Jesus, who we concluded earlier in Luke 19, is a man who was full of love and passion. This child was also prophesied in Isaiah 7, in the context of a war between Israel and Syria. War in the Middle East never ends! The more things change in the Middle East, the more they remain the same. Whether you read the Bible or the New York Times—it's always war in the Middle East: Syria at war with Israel; Iraq at war with Israel; Iran at war with Israel; the Palestinians at war with Israel! Nothing will ever change—or will it? God says things will change one day. God says he is going to send a special envoy—a Peacemaker. In Isaiah 7:10 God speaks to Ahaz, Israel's king, who is supposed to know the Lord; he is supposed to know better:

Ask the LORD your God for a sign, whether in the deepest depths or in the highest heights. But Ahaz said, "I will not ask; I will not put the LORD to the test." (Isaiah 7:10-12)

Self righteous and sanctimonious Ahaz basically said—I don't need to hear a word from God:

Then Isaiah said, "Hear now, you house of David! Is it not enough to try the patience of humans? Will you try the patience of my God also? Therefore the Lord himself will give you a sign: The virgin will conceive and give birth to a son, and will call him Immanuel." (Isaiah 7:13-14)

He is going to be an amazing child. He is going to be a marvel, a miracle child—God with us. And he is going to be the peacemaker that God brings to this world. The prophecy is, "For to us a child is born, to us a son is given (*Immanuel, the son of God*), and the **government will be on his shoulders**." (Isaiah 9: 6) This is referring, of course, to the second coming, when the Messiah is literally going to rule and reign in this world— now he rules spiritually in our hearts—but at this time, he will rule geopolitically. "And he will be called Wonderful Counselor, Mighty God, Everlasting Father, Prince of Peace..." Now notice this astounding resumé. This is more than a peace lover; this is more than a peacekeeper. This is the only one in the universe who can be a peacemaker. And do you know why? *Because whoever is going to make peace in this world is going to have to be smarter than anybody who ever lived!*

Resumé : Wonderful Counselor

And the first thing they said about this child who would be born is that he is going to have an IQ of infinity. It says, "He will be called *Wonderful Counselor*..." Listen to that. He is going to be the one who is a counselor and a wonder, a marvel, a miracle. The one who is going to have wisdom and insight and understanding that will be unparalleled in the history of human wisdom. He is going to have that kind of wisdom.

Now we have had a lot of wise and dedicated people who have tried to bring peace to the Middle East, and they have failed. We have a lot of committed, patriotic and very intelligent men and women working now around the clock with Colin Powell, who is one of the great champions and heroes of our nation, to try to bring peace. They are smart, dedicated, and patriotic. They are the best of the best—the crème de le crème—but even they can't establish world peace! As smart as they are—they are finite and limited. That's why, for instance, in our own wisdom, as we try to bring peace to the Middle East—we always fail! For example, when the UN took a vote a couple weeks ago to lift the sanctions against Sudan—a leading terrorist state—everybody voted for it! Sudan is literally ruled by Islamic fundamentalists who are terrorizing the nation, enslaving men, women and children in the Christian southern region. The United States, instead of voting against it, abstained from the vote. Why? Because we have to build a coalition of Arab nations to fight terrorism. And so we do the immoral thing—we just say to the Sudan, "That's Ok, you just go on your own way and keep enslaving all these people." Now do I say that because I'm not a patriot—or because I am trying to criticize our leaders and not support them? No, I'm behind them. But it was an immoral decision. Their wisdom had to play politics –sadly, and tragically. That's why we are willing to build an anti-terrorist coalition and even seek to get Iran and Syria on our side.

Iran! How can Iran be an ally—Hezbollah is controlled by Iran! How can Syria be an ally—Hamas works with Syria! The reason our nation makes these insane alliances is not because we are not dedicated to building a better world—we are. It's because we have absolutely no idea what to do. We don't have the wisdom to figure it all out. The truth is we can't figure it out and we never will—so we do the best we can. We choose the lesser of two evils. There's only one peacemaker with a truly brilliant mind—and we better learn to trust him quickly!

Resumé: Mighty God

Secondly, whoever is going to make peace in the Middle East better have a strong hand. He better have the greatest power, strength and influence of anyone who ever lived if he's going to bring peace to the Middle East. This will require the strongest hand that has ever been dealt in international politics. Isaiah 9:6 calls this individual "Wonderful Counselor and *Mighty God*..." Do you see that! *El Gibor*, the God who is a mighty, conquering hero. That is the name of this child who would be born and this son who would be given. His mind is infinitely wise and his power is omnipotent. It's going to take that kind of power to bring peace between Yasser Arafat and God, Ariel Sharon and God and Sharon and Arafat. If this is not the power that's at work, there's no hope—none. The United Nations has at times been very dedicated to seeking world peace. Nevertheless, I have real problems with the UN —big time problems. No one doubts that there are intelligent, committed individuals at the UN working hard in very difficult situations. But the fact is that the UN, like all of us, is fatally flawed. A few weeks ago in the International Racism Conference sponsored by the UN, the only nation in the entire world that the UN criticized for racism was Israel! Now that's amazing! Incredible! In light of all the terror that is directed at Israel by Islamic nations and terrorist organizations, along with all the other acts of terror perpetrated worldwide by Islamic and Communist nations, it is astonishing that at this UN sponsored conference on world racism—only Israel is singled out as a racist, terrorist nation!

Over the years the UN has accomplished some good things and at times has been well motivated. However, their credibility and effectiveness is now severely undermined by their virulent anti-Israel and anti-US worldview!

The United Nations began well. It was under UN auspices that Israel became a nation in 1948 in the aftermath of World War II. In the greatest conflict in the history of mankind, in which 50 million people died, out of the ashes of the Holocaust—Israel was reborn as a nation! The UN played a significant role in devising a two-state solution which respected the national aspirations of both Jews and Palestinians. The Jewish people would receive a homeland called Israel; and the Palestinians would receive a homeland called Palestine. It would also establish Jerusalem as an international city, with two capitals. It was a good plan and a noble effort. But on the very day that Israel became an independent nation— on that very day—the military forces of six Arab nations attacked them immediately. From the north came Syria and Lebanon—from the east came Iraq and Jordan—from the south came Saudi Arabia and Egypt. The

UN had a good plan, but there weren't enough statesmen, there weren't enough leaders to actually implement the good plan. But God says—my Messiah is coming and my plan will succeed where all others have failed because I am omniscient and I am omnipotent!

Now these are pretty impressive credentials—not a bad resumé!

Resumé: Everlasting Father

Thirdly, whoever is going to bring world peace will need to have more love than anyone else who ever lived—because you can't make peace in the midst of a world torn apart by hatred and violence without an extraordinary measure of wisdom, power and love. No love—no peace! No love—no reconciliation! Notice that this child to be born will be named "Wonderful Counselor, Mighty God, and *Everlasting Father*..." In Isaiah 9:6 the Hebrew designation for Everlasting Father is *Ab Ad,* meaning Father of Eternity. We know the word Abba which Jesus uses to refer to his Father in a very personal way. Isaiah wants us to understand that the Messiah will also love like the Father loves. Isaiah 9:6 is not saying that the Messiah is identical to the Father. We believe the Bible teaches clearly that there is only one God, and that this one true God reveals himself as God the Father, Son and Holy Spirit. Isaiah is saying that the Messiah is so intimately related to his Father that they are one. Seven hundred years later, Jesus says to the Jewish people: "I and my Father are one." (John 10:30) He means that the heart of *Abba,* the love of the Father, also characterizes the Son who would be born—and this love will last for eternity. Basically Isaiah is saying that someone is coming into the world with enough love to save it, to heal it, and to bring peace to it. That's one awesome resumé!

I was struck by the fact that at Ground Zero a few days ago, one of the brave rescue workers was coming out of the awful rubble, carefully and respectfully carrying the body of someone who had died. As he came out he looked up and right in front of him he saw a cross. It had been formed by the fractured steel beams as the towers collapsed. As the rescuer emerged from the wreckage and saw the cross, he said that he was overwhelmed by the image of the crucifixion. Yet he was greatly encouraged and rejoiced in the fact that this cross gave him new hope; that God knows our pain. What an awesome truth! No one has ever loved like that. And that's why Jesus the Messiah can be called the Prince of Peace—the *Sar-Shalom*. This is the Prince who brings to the world ultimate well-being—forgiveness, hope, comfort, security, blessedness, and incredible joy that endures the most difficult challenges of life. Happiness dies quickly, but *Shalom* lives forever because it's founded on the Messiah—on God himself—on God's great love.

So the fact is, there is someone who is coming with the passion and the resumé to establish peace—peace on earth and peace in human hearts.

SIGNS OF THE TIMES

I'm looking forward to that day. So where is He? How long will it be? Jesus himself reveals to us the signs of the times in Matthew 24, when his disciples asked him "when will this happen and what will be the sign of your coming and the end of the age?" (Vs. 2-3) Jesus answered them and said:

> Watch out that no one deceives you. For many will come in
> my name, claiming, "I am the Messiah" and will deceive many.
> (Matthew 24:4)

Jesus says the first sign of his coming is an exponential increase in religious cults, counterfeit messiahs and false religions. Now the world has had false religion since the Garden of Eden and Satan's deception. What Jesus meant was—when you are living in a day when false messiahs are proliferating, that's a sign that I'm coming back soon. Jesus means, ironically, that the darker the world gets, the closer he is to returning. This is the exact opposite of what many Christians are taught in their churches and seminaries—that the world is getting better, that Christianity is transforming the world for the better, and that we are building the kingdom for Jesus and when everything gets really great we will present it to him as a gift when he comes again. Now this optimistic scenario is not only naïve but entirely unbiblical. Anyone thinking objectively at all knows that we are not getting better. If the 20ᵗʰ and 21ˢᵗ centuries are the proof that we are *getting better,* then we need to redefine the word *better*. He said when you see false christs increasing—the end is near.

When you read the history of the world over the past 200 years, it is clear that there has been a tremendous increase in false religions and cults. A few days ago Sun Myung Moon was in New York City, the false prophet who says he is the Lord of the Second Advent. He actually claims to be the second coming of Jesus Christ. He says he is the second coming because Jesus failed and now he is here to succeed where Jesus failed. Jesus said when you see these imposters, these demonic preachers like Sun Myung Moon increasing—the coming of the true Messiah is near.

Jesus says there's a second sign:

> You will hear of wars and rumors of wars, but see to it that you are not alarmed. For nation shall rise against nation, and king-dom against kingdom... (Matthew 24:6-7)

We can now include the war against Islamic terrorism on this ugly list of world conflicts. Jesus says when you are living in the day and age when war is increasing dramatically—when more lives are being lost than ever before—then look up. The end is near. The darker the world gets, the closer *The Light of the World* is to returning.

Now if you enjoy studying history like I do, you know that war and violence have been the norm since Cain and Abel. But you also know that the 20ᵗʰ century was the most violent and deadly century in the history of the human race. More people were killed in war in this century than ever before. We are also the first generation in history to have the capability of destroying the entire human race through nuclear, biological and chemical weapons. But believe it or not, as hard as we try, God will not allow us to destroy ourselves and our world completely! God tells us that we have rejected him long enough and have tried to kill each other long enough. Now God says, "vengeance is Mine"—I will judge the world! What Jesus means is that when the human race has both the will and the means to destroy itself and God's world– look up, the end is near.

The third sign:

> There will be famines and earthquakes in various places. All these are the beginning of birth pains. (Matthew 24:12)

Jesus says when you see an increase in natural disasters—when you see "Mother Nature" more deadly than ever before—pay attention. Now of course we have had natural disasters since the great flood in Noah's day, and today is no different. We hear every day of earthquakes, tornados, hurricanes, floods, tsunamis, volcanic eruptions and horrific droughts resulting in awful famines. Today, perhaps more than ever before, we see nature as both the destroyer and the destroyed. Nature not only seems to be more deadly today than ever before—but also more broken and more endangered. In Romans 8 we read of the groaning of nature, the human race, and God himself—because all of creation longs to be reconciled to God.

There's a fourth sign:

> Then you will be handed over to be persecuted and put to death, and you will be hated by all nations because of Me. At that time many will turn away from the faith and will betray and hate each other, and many false prophets will appear and deceive many people. Because of the increase of wickedness, the love of most will grow cold, but the one who stands firm to the end will be saved. (Matthew 24:9-13)

Jesus says there will be an increase in the persecution of his people in the last days. If you are a student of the history of the church, you know that more people have given their lives for Christ in the 20th century than in all 19 previous centuries combined. The two greatest persecutors of Christians today are Islamic and communist nations. We are living in that day—today. The Lord is near. It's always darkest before the dawn.

And notice a fifth sign:

> And this gospel of the kingdom will be preached in the whole
> world as a testimony to all nations, and then the end will come.
> (Matthew 24:14)

Then the true Christ will come. We are living in the first generation in the history of the world that has the ability to communicate around the globe. We are the first generation of believers in Christ in the history of the church that literally has seen the gospel go to the four corners of the earth—via radio, satellite, the internet, and television. We are the first generation to ever see it. Glory to God. Even so come Lord Jesus.

Be encouraged—Jesus Christ has the passion and the resumé to bring peace to the world. The number one prophetic sign in the Bible concerning the last days is the re-gathering of the Jewish people and the rebirth of the nation Israel. Now after 2000 years of dispersion, in 1948, under the auspices of the world community and the United Nations, Israel became a nation again. We live in the generation that saw it happen! That's amazing.

Now notice Matthew 24:15

> So when you see standing in the holy place the abomination
> that causes desolation...

This is a shocking verse! We were just reading about the signs preceding the true Messiah's return to establish his kingdom—and suddenly we are talking about the *abomination of desolation*! The scriptures clearly teach that just before the end, just before Christ returns, God, for his own purpose, will allow a false christ to take power. He will be the last of the false messiahs to arise and his name will be the Antichrist! He will literally set up a government that will have enormous power in the world for seven years. He will actually dominate Israel and rule from Jerusalem for three and a half years. Most of the world will believe that he is the true messiah. He will almost certainly win the Nobel Peace Prize because he will make peace between the Palestinians and the Israelis.

A TIME *for* HOPE

In light of the insurmountable problems that dominate and threaten to destroy our world today, do you think the world is ready to embrace a counterfeit global savior? With the world becoming more of an inter-dependent global community day by day—how will we deal with war, nuclear weapons, terrorism, poverty, disease, the destruction of the environment, racism, genocide and the myriad other threats the human race faces on a daily basis? Is it possible that we are seeing the world stage set for the emergence of the Antichrist today? The Antichrist will have a very brief time on the world stage—he will have his 15 minutes of infamy—and then verse 29:

> Immediately after the distress of those days the sun will be darkened, and the moon will not give its light; the stars will fall from the sky, and the heavenly bodies will be shaken. Then will appear the **sign of the Son of Man** in heaven. And then **all the peoples of the earth will mourn** when they see the Son of Man coming on the clouds of heaven, with power and great glory. And he will send his angels with a loud trumpet call, and they will gather his elect from the four winds, from one end of the heavens to the other. (Matthew 24:29-31)

Jesus Christ will return and establish his kingdom and remake the world the way it was created and redeemed to be! The prophet Isaiah was given a vision of this awesome Messianic kingdom:

> In the last days the mountain of the LORD's temple will be established as the highest of the mountains; it will be exalted above the hills, and all nations will stream to it. Many peoples will come and say, "Come, let us go up to the mountain of the LORD, to the temple of the God of Jacob. He will teach us his ways, so that we may walk in his paths. The law will go out from Zion, the word of the LORD from Jerusalem. He (*the Messiah Jesus*) will judge between the nations and will settle disputes for many peoples. They will beat their swords into plowshares and their spears into pruning hooks. Nation will

not take up sword against nation, nor will they train for war anymore. Come, descendants of Jacob, let us walk in the light of the LORD." (Isaiah 2:2-5)

This King and kingdom are coming. The United Nations actually has Isaiah 2:4 inscribed on the Isaiah wall in New York City, but unfortunately the UN forgets the context—which is the return of the true Messiah, Jesus Christ, to rule the world with love and justice. Then, and only then, will the prophecy be fulfilled that, "Nation will not take up sword against nation, nor will they train for war anymore."

If you are here today and are not experiencing "peace *with* God"; if you are still at war *with* God, Romans 5:1 says, "Therefore, since we have been justified through faith, we have peace with God..." Our war with God is over. Isn't it awesome to know that although we declared war on God, he declared peace on us! God could have annihilated us in a heartbeat, and would have had every spiritual, moral and legal right to do so. Instead, he made peace with us through the sacrifice of his Son Jesus Christ on the cross. Have you ever thanked God for this indescribable gift? Have you ever asked Jesus Christ to forgive you and set you free? I urge you today to repent of your sins and submit yourself to Jesus Christ as the ruler of your life. Then you will have "peace *with* God" and begin to experience the "peace *of* God." That's why the Apostle Paul exhorts us in Philippians 4:6-7:

> Do not be anxious about anything, but in every situation, by prayer and petition, with thanksgiving, present your requests to God. And the ***peace of God***, which transcends all understanding, will guard your hearts and your minds in Christ Jesus.

When you pray about everything, God will give you peace about everything! He will keep your thoughts and emotions from stressing you beyond your strength. Take hold of the God of peace by faith right now.

Those who experience peace with God and the peace of God are then qualified to be peacemakers. Jesus said, "Blessed are the peacemakers for they shall be called the children of God." (Matthew 5:9) God wants us to be instruments of peace in our families, in our workplace, in our community, in our church, in our nation, and in our world. Let's ask God to make us more than peace lovers and peacekeepers—let's ask him to make us peacemakers! Our prayer should be: God, use me to bring enemies together; use me to be an instrument of active goodwill where there has only been malice and hatred. If we are willing to pray that prayer, God will honor that prayer—but it will cost us.

Let's also remember to "pray for the peace of Jerusalem." King David invites us in Psalm 122 to:

> Pray for the peace of Jerusalem: "May those who love you be secure. May there be peace within your walls and security within your citadels." For the sake of my family and friends, I will say, "Peace be within you." For the sake of the house of the LORD our God, I will seek your prosperity. (Psalm 122:6-9)

In the name of God the Father and God the Son and God the Holy Spirit. Amen.

PART II

Terrorism:
The Apostle Paul

CHAPTER 5
Confessions of a Terrorist

9/11 changed the world. The focus is now on understanding and defeating Islamic terrorism. Can the Bible help?

Much of the New Testament was written by a Jewish rabbi and Pharisee named Saul. He was a terrorist. Eventually, he became a new man—a Jewish Christian apostle, full of love instead of hate, named Paul. He explains his radical change of heart and life in his "confessions" in Acts 22:1-10, before a Jewish crowd who used to love him and now wants him dead:

> Brothers and fathers, listen now to my defense. When they heard him speak to them in Aramaic, they became very quiet. Then Paul said: "I am a Jew, born in Tarsus of Cilicia, but brought up in this city. I studied under Gamaliel and was thoroughly trained in the law of our ancestors. I was just as zealous for God as any of you are today. I persecuted the followers of this Way to their death, arresting both men and women and throwing them into prison, as the high priest and all the Council can themselves testify. I even obtained letters from them to their associates in Damascus, and went there to bring these people as prisoners to Jerusalem to be punished. About noon as I came near Damascus, suddenly a bright light from heaven

flashed around me. I fell to the ground and heard a voice say to me, "Saul! Saul! Why do you persecute me?"

"Who are you, Lord?" I asked.

"I am Jesus of Nazareth, whom you are persecuting," he replied. "My companions saw the light, but they did not understand the voice of him who was speaking to me."

"What shall I do, Lord?" I asked.

"Get up," the Lord said, "and go into Damascus. There you will be told all that you have been assigned to do."

It's rare to ever hear a terrorist confess his crimes—much less for one to experience a genuine spiritual conversion. In our world there are too many terrorists, too few confessions, and too few conversions.

✦ We have ***adolescent terrorists*** like Eric Harris and Dylan Klebold at Columbine High School engaging in cold blooded murder and suicide.

✦ We have ***political terrorists*** like the Unabomber Ted Kaczynski, Timothy McVeigh who bombed the Murrah Federal Building in Oklahoma City, and Eric Rudolph who bombed the Atlanta Olympics and committed murder at an abortion clinic. Rudolph is often described as a *"Christian"* terrorist, but he claims Nietzsche as his hero, not Jesus Christ. In a September 2005 article in Christianity Today he said, "They (*Christian*s) have been so nice; I would hate to break it to them that I really prefer Nietzsche to the Bible— because they are 'good people, mostly born-again Christians, looking to save my soul.'" Political terrorists are sometimes found among the Nihilists, Anarchists, and Antinomians.

✦ We have *racial terrorists* like Edgar Killen of the Ku Klux Klan—who was also a part-time Baptist preacher! He escaped justice in the 1960's when one juror said she could never, ever convict a preacher! He was involved in the killing of the three brave civil rights workers in Mississippi. Finally justice was done. A local report said that, "The KKK killer gets 60 years for triple slayings." The judge said, "Each life has value." He sentenced former KKK leader Edgar Ray Killen to the maximum 60 years in prison for masterminding the 1964 slayings of civil rights workers. Killen, a part-time Baptist minister, has expressed no remorse, no confessions. The attorney general said, "I know at some point he will get to that realization—you don't get to heaven unless you admit what you have done and ask for forgiveness. He's 80 years old so I can imagine that's a death sentence." Thank God for some justice.

✦ We have *religious terrorists* like Mohammed Atta and his Islamic brothers. Nineteen murderers all claiming to serve Allah, 15 of them from Saudi Arabia, the birthplace of Mohammed and the location of Islam's two holiest sites—Mecca and Medina. Not all Muslims are terrorists, but all the 9/11 terrorists were Muslim.

Two thousand years ago there was the Jewish *religious terrorist* Saul of Tarsus, who confessed his crimes before King Agrippa in Acts 26:9-11:

I too was convinced that *I ought* to do all that was possible to oppose the name of Jesus of Nazareth. And that is just what I did in Jerusalem. On the authority of the chief priests I put many of the Lord's people in prison, and when they were put to death, I cast my vote against them. Many a time I went from one synagogue to another to have them punished, and I tried to force them to blaspheme. I was so obsessed with persecuting them that I even hunted them down in foreign cities.

The ultimate expression of religious terrorism is murder in the name of God! The Bible records the confessions of a terrorist. It is a relevant passage of Scripture to study as we wage spiritual warfare against terrorism.

So how do we fight and defeat terrorism? Is there an answer? I was in India a few years ago during their Independence Day. I was greatly impressed by a young 10th grade school girl as she gave a powerful speech on why terrorism is the greatest threat to India's freedom and security:

> How does the shedding of innocent blood and the wailing of widowed women and orphaned children—become "holy" war? It's high time we condemn their actions in the strongest terms. Terrorism in any form must be wiped off the face of the earth!

> If religion doesn't teach us to be tolerant and respectful, it is better to be an atheist. If our faith generates narrow-mindedness and ill-feeling toward our fellow human beings, it is nothing other than fundamentalism or fanaticism.

Not long after this heartfelt expression and Independence Day celebration, Mumbai, India was struck by a horrific Islamic terrorist attack in July 2006. Is anyone listening?

So what is the solution to terrorism? How do we "wipe it off the face of the earth?"

✦ There is the *military response*. This option is being pursued in the wars in Afghanistan and Iraq. We honor the nearly 5,000 courageous American military men and women and those from other nations who have made the ultimate sacrifice in the war on terror. We remember the nearly 3,000 men, women and children from the United States and many other nations who were murdered on 9/11. We also acknowledge the people of Afghanistan and Iraq who are fighting and dying for their freedom against Islamic terrorists.

Regardless of your personal politics concerning the war in Iraq and President Bush, there was a very poignant exchange between the President and a 4th grade girl whose father is in the military. She wrote the President a letter which said, "Dear Mr. President, As much as I don't want my dad to fight, I am willing to give him to you." The President responded to her privately, but also provided this public response, "This young girl knows what America is all about. Since September 11th, an entire generation of young Americans has gained new understanding of the value of freedom, and its cost, and duty, and its sacrifice." The military option is necessary and effective, but it is costly—the price is paid in the blood of brave young men and women.

✦ There is the ***political response.*** This is the ongoing response of the United Nations and the international community. Sadly, even though this response is often well intended, because of the suffocating political correctness, and the often underlying anti-Israel and anti-US posture, this response is woefully inadequate and ineffective. The reason I don't have much faith in this option is *because the U.N. assigns terrorist nations to monitor world terrorism!* It makes a thinking person wonder if the whole world has gone mad!

✦ There is the ***economic response.*** Some nations are freezing terrorist assets and placing economic sanctions against other nations which are supporting terrorism. This is a necessary and effective option.

✦ There is the need for an ***educational response.*** Every nation needs to teach its children respect for all human

life and for the beauty of diverse cultures. We only need to observe the devastating effects of Wahhabism in Saudi Arabia and the Middle East. Adults are poisoning children with religious hate, a perverted sense of history, and encouraging them to murder and destroy the Jews, the nation of Israel, and its friends and allies. They are also encouraging their children to kill themselves in suicide/homicide bomb attacks—what a grotesque and ungodly educational system! Is Allah really pleased with this? Is it a coincidence that 15 of 19 terrorist highjackers were Saudis? No chance!

✦ There is the *religious response.* It is imperative that all religious leaders—including Muslim clerics—repudiate terrorism, hatred and murder! The response of Muslim leadership in the first few years after 9/11 was abysmal! It was shameful! For too long their political leaders, the legal profession, religious leaders, the intelligentsia and media, the arts community and others were deafeningly silent! Where are the "moderate" voices that reject murder and terror? For too long there has been a sickening silence—or at best an occasional mild rebuke of Islamic terrorism with the caveat that the Jews are evil and Israel needs to be destroyed and the US is Satan. This is not an effective religious response to terrorism! Only more recently has there been any courage and righteousness displayed publically by some Muslim leaders. I was interested in an effort by one US Muslim leader, Sahid Sahid, to take a strong stand against terrorism. He is the Secretary General of the Islamic Society of North America. He was quoted as saying:

> Muslims worldwide have been under renewed
> pressure to distance themselves from extrem-

ists after a summer of deadly terrorist attacks in London and in Egypt and insurgent assaults on civilians and coalition troops in Iraq. The Islamic society based in Plainfield (Indiana) has joined other Muslims in repeatedly denouncing terrorism.

Well, that's good. Its way overdue, but it's good! If he and his organization are genuinely against terrorism—may their tribe increase! Sahid ended with these words:

This group ISNA tries to underscore its opposition to the radical interpretation of Islam by helping organize American Muslim scholars to issue a religious edict or a fatwa condemning terrorism in July. The convention will continue that conversation by discussing the fatwa and asking attendees to sign a pledge against extremism. We have never been in this fatwa business. It dispels some misunderstanding. We should do whatever it takes.

And if he is sincere, and only time will tell—he is right on!

We need these various options. All of these responses to terrorism are **necessary**, but they are **not sufficient**! The only final solution to the Islamic terror problem is a **spiritual** one (not religious, but spiritual)—human hearts and minds must be transformed by the love and power of God! Terrorists must become new people with a new beginning, a personal renaissance, a new birth! Every terrorist, Muslim and otherwise, needs to encounter Jesus Christ and be set free by the gospel—just like the terrorist Saul. Standing before King Agrippa years later, the Apostle Paul, formerly known as the terrorist Saul, testified to his miraculous transformation:

On one of these journeys I was going to Damascus with the authority and commission of the chief priests. About noon,

A Time *for* Hope

King Agrippa, as I was on the road, I saw a light from heaven, brighter than the sun, blazing around me and my companions. We all fell to the ground, and I heard a voice saying to me in Aramaic, "Saul, Saul, why do you persecute me? It is hard for you to kick against the goads."

Then I asked, "Who are you, Lord?"

"I am Jesus, whom you are persecuting," the Lord replied. "Now get up and stand on your feet. I have appeared to you to appoint you as a servant and as a witness of what you have seen and will see of me. I will rescue you from your own people and from the Gentiles. I am sending you to them to open their eyes and turn them from darkness to light, and from the power of Satan to God, so that they may receive forgiveness of sins and a place among those who are sanctified by faith in me." (Acts 26:13-18)

Do you know what Paul's life proves? God hates terrorism but he loves terrorists! God's power and grace transforms a man full of hate and murder into a man filled with love and compassion. Notice Paul's response:

So then, King Agrippa, I was not disobedient to the vision from heaven. First to those in Damascus, then to those in Jerusalem and in all Judea, and then to the Gentiles, I preached that they should repent and turn to God and demonstrate their repentance by their deeds. (Acts 26:19-20)

Clearly, the ultimate option and response to terrorism is the love and power of God! Human hearts and minds have to be changed! This is the only sufficient solution. Paul knew this powerful truth firsthand. It is Jesus Christ who sets the terrorist free. John records the following account of Jesus preaching to the Jewish people about freedom:

Even as he spoke, many believed in him. To the Jews who had believed him, Jesus said, "If you hold to my teaching, you are really my disciples. Then you will know the truth, and the truth will set you free."

They answered him, "We are Abraham's descendants and have never been slaves of anyone. How can you say that we shall be set free?"

Jesus replied, "Very truly I tell you, everyone who sins is a slave to sin. Now a slave has no permanent place in the family, but a son belongs to it forever. So if the Son sets you free, you will be free indeed." (John 8:30-36)

Jesus teaches that the ultimate freedom is from slavery and the greatest slave master of all is sin. Then Jesus promises that when he sets us free from whatever controls us—and terrorism is an evil and grotesque sin—then we will be truly free.

There are many places in the New Testament where Paul gives his testimony of conversion and also confesses his sin of terrorism. We need to understand how relevant this truth is for such a time as this in our history. We need to understand how Paul came to realize that his only hope to become a new man was the grace of God! Paul says to his young disciple Timothy:

I thank Christ Jesus our Lord, who has given me strength, that he considered me trustworthy, appointing me to his service—even though I was once a blasphemer and a persecutor and a violent man.... (1 Timothy 1:12-13)

Paul confesses his terrorism and then he says:

I was shown mercy because I acted in ignorance and unbelief. The grace of our Lord was poured out on me abundantly, along with the faith and love that are in Christ Jesus. Here is a trustworthy saying that deserves full acceptance: Christ Jesus came into the world to save sinners—of whom I am the worst. But for that very reason I was shown mercy so that in me, the worst of sinners, Christ Jesus might display his immense patience as an example for those who would believe in him and receive eternal life. (1Timothy 1:14-16)

Then he ends with the most beautiful doxology:

Now to the King eternal, immortal, invisible, the only God, be honor and glory for ever and ever. Amen. (1Timothy 1:17)

THE MIND OF A TERRORIST

It's time now to climb into the mind of a terrorist—and the mind of a terrorist is a terrible place to be. But it displays a large degree of order and reason. Terrorists are made, not born. And the Apostle Paul, the former terrorist, was no exception. So what does he want us to know about his life as a terrorist to help us better understand and confront terrorism?

Upbringing and Theological Training

First, Paul wants us to know that the seeds of his terrorism were planted in his upbringing and theological training. He gives us an inside look at this truth as he speaks before King Agrippa in Acts 26:4-5:

The Jewish people all know the way I have lived ever since I was a child, from the beginning of my life in my own country, and also in Jerusalem. They have known me for a long time and can testify, if they are willing, that I conformed to the strict-est sect of our religion, living as a Pharisee.

It's important to Paul, as he confesses his crimes and gives his testimony, to start at the beginning. He emphasizes that he was impacted profoundly since his earliest childhood, and it resulted in an utter conformity to the strictest expectations of his religion. Earlier Paul had responded to a hostile Jewish crowd by speaking of his prior religious zeal and training:

> I am a Jew, born in Tarsus of Cilicia, but brought up in this city.
> I studied under Gamaliel and was ***thoroughly trained in the
> law of our ancestors***. I was just as ***zealous for God*** as any of
> you are today. (Acts 22:3)

The New King James version translates Paul's words about being
"thoroughly trained" as "I was taught in the strictness of my fathers."
The word "taught" is from the Greek word *paideuo*, from which we get
the English word pedagogy—the art and science of teaching, nourishing,
training and bringing up children. Paul is saying that this religious system
in which he was trained ultimately inspired a zeal for God which became
perverted and motivated him to hate and kill the enemies of God!

Paul links his religious zealotry to his intense religious training. The
fearful and terrible results are then explained to the crowd:

> I persecuted the followers of this Way to their death, arresting
> both men and women and throwing them into prison, as the
> high priest and all the Council can themselves testify. I even
> obtained letters from them to their associates in Damascus, and
> went there to bring these people as prisoners to Jerusalem to be
> punished. (Acts 22:4-5)

John MacArthur has an interesting comment on Paul's religious training.

> As a student of Gamaliel, Paul received extensive training in
> the Old Testament law, and in the rabbinic traditions. (The
> MacArthur Study Bible, pg. 1676)

In Jewish education the rabbinic traditions reflected in the Talmud and
the opinions of the rabbis often take precedence over biblical truth itself—
encouraging a sense of religious superiority and legalistic righteousness.
Paul knew firsthand how this system, which often gave more weight to
the words of men than to the words of God, ended up turning the traditions of men into the law of God! He knew how poisonous that system
had been in driving him to hurt the enemies of God in order to honor his

religious tradition. Terrorists get all the tradition and miss all the truth! Paul reflects upon this deadly religious tradition in Philippians 3:4-6:

> Further, my brothers and sisters, rejoice in the Lord! It is no trouble for me to write the same things to you again, and it is a safeguard for you. Watch out for those dogs, those evildoers, those mutilators of the flesh.

Paul uses some really harsh language. You might ask—"Was this a personal attack?" Of course it was—but he had a reason. He is talking about those who were practicing circumcision in a way that equated religious tradition with righteousness. Paul is saying that people don't get right with God by physical circumcision but by believing in God's Son for mercy and forgiveness.

> For it is we who are the circumcision, we who serve God by his Spirit, who boast in Christ Jesus, and who put no confidence in the flesh—though I myself have reasons for such confidence. If someone else thinks they have reasons to put confidence in the flesh, I have more: circumcised on the eighth day, of the people of Israel, of the tribe of Benjamin, a Hebrew of Hebrews; in regard to the law, a Pharisee; as for zeal, persecuting the church; as for righteousness based on the law, faultless.

Basically, Paul is saying—check me out. If you want to talk about legalistic righteousness—how about "circumcised on the eighth day." I don't remember it but I know it happened! As for righteousness—I am faultless! Paul knew the religious environment which breeds arrogance, fundamentalism and intolerance. It's present in every religion!

Paul shares more insight into his religious background in Galatians 1:13-14. Galatians was written to Christians who had started well, by trusting in God's grace, but were now trusting in their own efforts to achieve spiritual maturity. Paul continues his confessions by saying:

For you have heard of my previous way of life in Judaism, how intensely I persecuted the church of God and tried to destroy it. *I was advancing* in Judaism beyond many of my own age among my people and was *extremely zealous* for the traditions of my fathers.

Paul is saying—was I climbing the career ladder or what! During his years as a Pharisee, Paul had been tragically ignorant of the destructive consequences of elevating religious tradition above biblical truth. Jesus himself, however, was not ignorant of the devastating impact. In Matthew 23 Jesus reserves his greatest condemnation for religious leaders who kill people physically and spiritually, driven by their pride, hypocrisy, arrogance, lies, and greed.

Then Jesus said to the crowds and to his disciples: The teachers of the law and the Pharisees sit in Moses' seat.

So you must be careful to do everything they tell you. *But do not do what they do, for they do not practice what they preach*. They tie up heavy, cumbersome loads and put them on other people's shoulders, but they themselves are not willing to lift a finger to move them...

Woe to you, teachers of the law and Pharisees, you hypocrites! You shut the door of the kingdom of heaven in people's faces. You yourselves do not enter, nor will you let those enter who are trying to. Woe to you, teachers of the law and Pharisees, you hypocrites! You travel over land and sea to win a single convert, and when you have succeeded, you make them twice as much a child of hell as you are...

Woe to you, teachers of the law and Pharisees, you hypocrites! You are like whitewashed tombs, which look beautiful on the outside but on the inside are full of the bones of the dead and everything unclean. In the same way, on the outside you appear to people as righteous but on the inside you are full of hypocrisy and wickedness.

Woe to you, teachers of the law and Pharisees, you hypocrites! You build tombs for the prophets and decorate the graves of the righteous. And you say, "If we had lived in the days of our ancestors, we would not have taken part with them in shedding the blood of the prophets." So you testify against yourselves that you are the descendants of those who murdered the prophets. Go ahead, then, and complete what your ancestors started!

You snakes! You brood of vipers! How will you escape being condemned to hell? Therefore I am sending you prophets and sages and teachers. Some of them you will kill and crucify; others you will flog in your synagogues and pursue from town to town. And so upon you will come all the righteous blood that has been shed on earth, from the blood of righteous Abel to the blood of Zechariah son of Berekiah, whom you murdered between the temple and the altar. Truly I tell you, all this will come on this generation.

Jerusalem, Jerusalem, you who kill the prophets and stone those sent to you, how often I have longed to gather your children together, as a hen gathers her chicks under her wings, and you were not willing. Look, your house is left to you desolate. For I tell you, you will not see me again until you say, "Blessed is he who comes in the name of the Lord." (Matthew 23:1-4, 13-15, 27-38)

This proud rejection of biblical truth and the embracing of religious tradition in its place continues in our day, among Christians, Muslims, Jews, Hindus, Buddhists and others. Occasionally we have had a number of our Orthodox Jewish neighbors protest in front of Calvary Baptist Church in New York City, where I have pastored these past 14 years. The reason often given for the protests is that we work together with Jewish

Christian ministries such as Jews for Jesus, Chosen People, and Word of Messiah to offer the gospel to Jewish people. We are often accused of deception because we invite Jewish people to receive Jesus as their Messiah and assure them that they don't stop being Jewish when they become followers of Yeshua Hamashiach, Jesus the Messiah. On one particular day, I was discussing the Old Testament prophets with one of the Jewish Rabbis who is a leader in the counter-missionary movement. As we talked, his rabbinical students were listening, even as the rabbis prepared for a press conference on a New York City sidewalk, right in front of my church. I said, "Rabbi, your prophets in the Bible tell us that the Messiah will be born to a virgin, and do miracles, and live a sinless life, and die for mankind's sins and rise from the dead—and Yeshua fulfilled all the scriptures." And the rabbi, without hesitation, in front of all his students, shouted out to me, "I don't care what the Bible says—I care what the rabbis say!" The rabbi had brought his students to picket our church, and as the crowd grew, and the press conference was about to begin, the students held up their signs which said—*Stop Converting Jews* and *We Don't Need Saving*. During the press conference the Rabbi literally accused us as Christians of stealing Jewish children from their mothers and said that if a Jewish person trusted in Jesus, that person ceased to be Jewish! So I asked the Rabbi, "Are you still looking for the hope and consolation of Israel?" And he said, "Yes, I am." And so I asked him, "And when Messiah comes—will you believe in Him?" And he said, "Yes, I will." And so then I asked, "So Rabbi, when Messiah comes and you believe in him—will you cease to be Jewish?" The Rabbi was silent. Then he said, "No, I will not cease to be Jewish." So I asked him, "Then why do you insist that those Jews who believe in Yeshua as Messiah cease to be Jewish?" And the Rabbi had no answer. This is just one example of the mindset and attitude present in every religion, when corrupt religious tradition is allowed to override and veto biblical truth!

And this is the religious pride, hypocrisy, arrogance, legalism and fundamentalism that gave rise to the Pharisee Saul's terrorism 2000 years ago—and if left unchecked will inspire every form of religious terrorism today in 2011—of which Islamic terrorism is the most heinous, graphic and dangerous example.

In Islamic terrorism today:

+ There is the conviction that Islam is supreme and destined to world dominance through jihad for Allah's glory.

+ There is an intense hatred of Israel and the Jews and a total commitment to their utter destruction.

+ There is a willful corruption of the history of Israel and the Middle East.

+ There is the brutal use of the Palestinians as political pawns.

+ There is the grotesque offering of their own children as "*martyrs*" and homicide/suicide bombers. (It's often been said that peace will come to the Middle East when Islamic terrorists begin to love their children more than they hate Jewish children).

What are we teaching our children? What example are we showing them? What legacy are we leaving them? Children become terrorists because they are taught to hate and encouraged to kill. Whether it's Islamic terror, the Christian political terror of Northern Ireland, the Hindu Nationalist terror of India, the racial terror of the Ku Klux Klan in the United States, or the ancient terror of the Pharisee Saul, the recipe is always the same—when religious tradition trumps biblical truth, the potential for religious terrorism grows exponentially!

The Nobel Prize winner and Holocaust survivor Eli Wiesel illustrates this terrible truth in comments he made about the death of Simon Wiesenthal:

Simon Wiesenthal, the Nazi hunter, died this past week. He also suffered himself in concentration camps. In the Washington Post they were talking about his life and it said, "Wiesenthal, himself, was rounded up with other Jews and nearly

killed by Ukrainian soldiers (before he ever went to a concentration camp). Each of these Jewish prisoners stood against
a wall and beside a wooden crate that was meant to hold a
corpse. An officer shot a man in the neck, swigged liquor and
then shot the next man. As the officer approached Wiesenthal
the church bells sounded and the officer said, 'Enough, it's
time for evening mass.'"

The Apostle Paul has warned us—the seeds of his terrorism were
planted in his upbringing and his religious education.

Hatred and Murder

Secondly, Paul tells us that he came to believe that he served God
best by hating and destroying God's enemies. Paul had mentioned to the
crowd in Acts 22:3-4:

> I was thoroughly trained in the law of our Fathers and was just
> as *zealous* for God as any of you are today. *I persecuted the
> follows of this Way to their death*...

He told King Agrippa in Acts 26:9 that "I was convinced I *ought* to do
everything possible to oppose the name of Jesus..." Paul literally understood
that it was his religious obligation and duty to hate and destroy Christians!
He understood hatred and murder to be a spiritual and moral imperative!

Jesus warns his followers that people like Saul will actually believe
they are serving God when they kill Christians. In John 16:1-4 Jesus pre-
dicts the coming religious persecution:

> All this I have told you so that you will not fall away. They will
> put you out of the synagogue; in fact, the *time is coming when
> anyone who kills you will think they are offering a service to
> God*. They will do such things because they have not known the
> Father or me. I have told you this, so that when their time comes
> you will remember that I warned you about them...

A Time *for* Hope

Islamic terrorists today ceremonially cleanse themselves before they serve Allah by committing murder. They pray before they kill. As they kill they cry out, "Allahu Akbar—God is great!"

Daniel Pipes is one of the world's most insightful analysts of terrorism in the Middle East. In an article entitled *Christianity is Dying in It's Birthplace* he argues that the reason for this is Islamic terrorism, particularly seen in Palestinian Muslims who are persecuting Palestinian Christians. He then sites a specific incident:

> What some observers are calling a Pogrom took place near Ramallah on the West Bank on the night of September 4th. That's when 15 Muslim youths from one village, Dair Jarir, rampaged against Taybah, a nearly all Christian village of 1500 people. The reason for the assault? A Muslim woman from Dair Jarir, Hiyam Ajaj, 23 years old, fell in love with her Christian boss, Mehdi Khouriyye. He was the owner of a tailor shop in the Christian village. The couple maintained a clandestine 2 year affair and she became pregnant in March of 2005. When her family members learned of her condition they murdered her (about September 1st). Unsatisfied even with this honor killing—for Islamic law strictly forbids non Muslim males to have sexual relations with Muslim females—the men from the Muslim village sought vengeance against this Christian man and his family. According to the Catholic Custodian of the Holy Land, Pierbattista Pizzaballa, "Almost every day our communities are harassed by the Islamic extremists in these regions and if it is not the members of Hamas or Islamic Jihad, there are clashes with the Palestinian authority." In addition to the Islamists, a Muslim Land Mafia is said to operate with Palestinian authority complicity. It threatens Christian land and house owners, often succeeding to compel them to abandon their properties.

Daniel Pipes makes an interesting point about why there hasn't been more effectiveness in dissuading the Palestinian Muslims from persecuting the Christian Palestinians. He says:

> One factor that would help prevent this dismal outcome would be for our mainline protestant churches to speak out against Palestinian Muslims for tormenting and expelling Palestinian Christians. To date, unfortunately however, the Episcopalian, the Evangelical Lutheran, the Methodist, the Presbyterian and the United Church of Christ have ignored the problem.

Islamic terrorists sincerely believe that they are honoring Mohammad their prophet and Allah their God when they destroy their enemies. Contrast this evil mindset with the teaching of Jesus in Matthew 26:47-52:

> While he was still speaking, Judas, one of the Twelve, arrived. With him was a large crowd armed with swords and clubs, sent from the chief priests and the elders of the people. Now the betrayer had arranged a signal with them: "The one I kiss is the man; arrest him." Going at once to Jesus, Judas said, "Greetings, Rabbi!" and kissed him. Jesus replied, "Do what you came for, friend." Then the men stepped forward, seized Jesus and arrested him. With that, one of Jesus' companions reached for his sword, drew it out and struck the servant of the high priest, cutting off his ear. Put your sword back in its place," Jesus said to him, "for all who draw the sword will die by the sword."

Mohammad commands his followers to commit violence in jihad. Jesus rebukes his followers for using violence even to protect Him! Throughout history there have been Muslims and Christians who have responded to their enemies with hatred and violence. The huge difference is, of course, when Christians respond in such an evil manner, their response is a direct contradiction of both the life and the teaching of Jesus Christ. When Muslims respond in this violent manner, their response is consistent with the life and teaching of Mohammad. The contrast could not be more graphic.

A TIME *for* HOPE

The Apostle John highlights this contrast when he speaks about the power and necessity of love:

> Beloved, let us love one another, for love is of God; and everyone who loves is born of God and knows God. He who does not love does not know God, for God is love. In this the love of God was manifested toward us, that God has sent his only begotten Son into the world that we might live through him. In this is love, not that we loved God, but that he loves us and sent his son to be the propitiation for our sins. Beloved, if God so loved us, we also ought to love one another. (1 John 4:7-11)

And of course John learned about love from Jesus! In the greatest sermon ever preached, the Sermon on the Mount, Jesus encourages his followers to love and bless their enemies, not to hate and destroy them:

> You have heard that it was said, 'Love your neighbor and hate your enemy.' But I tell you, love your enemies and pray for those who persecute you, that you may be children of your Father in heaven. He causes his sun to rise on the evil and the good, and sends rain on the righteous and the unrighteous. If you love those who love you, what reward will you get? Are not even the tax collectors doing that? And if you greet only your own people, what are you doing more than others? Do not even pagans do that? Be perfect, therefore, as your heavenly Father is perfect. (Matthew 5:43-48)

The New York Times just reported this week that a Muslim chaplain with the New York City Fire Department resigned yesterday. Imam Intikab Habib resigned amidst a firestorm of controversy after "publicly doubting that 19 highjackers were responsible for the September 11th attacks" and "suggesting that the World Trade Center collapse was part of a conspiracy." Remember what we learned about Saul: the way you justify violence against the so called enemies of God is by perverting history and getting other people to believe in your perversion! You are seeing it in New York today! This chaplain said, "there are so many conflicting reports about 9/11 that I don't believe it was 19 highjackers who did those attacks. Was it 19 highjackers or was it a conspiracy?" Later in the article he says, "It takes 2 or 3 weeks to demolish a building like that with fire alone, but it was pulled down in a couple of hours." To his credit, I think he did say that the events of 9/11 were a tragedy. Of course, this is not a disavowal of terrorism. Then the editorial says this, "What we find most significant about Habib is that he is a Guyanese native and spent 6 years in Saudi Arabia studying Islamic theology and law before immigrating here in 2000." Now remember that 15 of the 19 highjackers were from Saudi Arabia. Given his 9/11 conspiracy theory, it suggests that he was thoroughly steeped in the Wahabi extremism originating in that country. It was Wahabism that spawned the group that conducted the 9/11 terrorist attacks, no matter what Habib believes. New York Senator Chuck Schummer said that the massive Saudi funded propagation of Wahabism is the root cause of terrorism. It reinforces the truth, which is found in all religions that become terroristic, that the source of terrorism is always about how we are raised, what we are taught, how we are encouraged to live, how we define salvation, and what it means to serve God.

Obsession

The third thing Paul tells us is that his desire to destroy God's enemies became his obsession and his purpose for living. Paul told King Agrippa in Acts 26:11 that "I was so *obsessed* with persecuting them (Christians) that I *even* hunted them down in foreign cities." Paul's obsession was a single-minded goal, driven by an overwhelming rage, against the perceived enemies of God. This obsession drove Saul (Paul) to force Jewish Christians to blaspheme Jesus Christ, to punish them, to imprison them, and ultimately to execute them.

A couple of months ago I was preaching in London. At one of the churches the pastor asked me to give a message on terrorism and the need for the gospel—especially because of what had happened in New York City. He said that he really felt that London was going to be hit next. His statement was prophetic for sure because they were attacked a short time later!

Omar Khyam was the ringleader behind the London homicide/suicide bombings on July 7th which attacked trains and buses and killed 56 people. He made a farewell video in which he described himself as a soldier of war and warned of future terror attacks. He said, "We will not stop this fight."

Khyam said he is inspired by Al Qaeda leader Osama Bin Laden and Zarqawi, who is suspected of ordering terror attacks in Iraq. Khyam ends his video by saying, "I and thousands like me are forsaking everything for what we believe."

Omar Khaym was married with a 14-month-old daughter. He had so much to live for, yet he says that the obsession of his life was to hate and kill God's enemies. It was to destroy everyone who opposed Allah. He said he would kill and be killed in jihad—he and thousands like him.

The Pharisee Saul knew exactly what that obsession was about!

I am so glad to be a follower of Christ and not a follower of Mohammad. We have been contrasting the hate and murder of religious terrorists with the love of Jesus Christ. You can tell when and where God's Word is really having an impact because it produces love in people. In 1 John 2:5-11 we read:

> But if anyone obeys his word, love for God is truly made complete in them. This is how we know we are in him: Whoever claims to live in him must live as Jesus did.

> Dear friends, I am not writing you a new command but an old one, which you have had since the beginning. This old command is the message you have heard. Yet I am writing you a new command; its truth is seen in him and in you, because the darkness is passing and the true light is already shining.

> Anyone who claims to be in the light but hates a brother or sister is still in the darkness. Anyone who loves their brother and sister

lives in the light, and there is nothing in them to make them stumble. But anyone who hates a brother or sister is in the darkness and walks around in the darkness. They do not know where they are going, because the darkness has blinded them.

Paul tells us that before God's love transformed him, his life was an obsession with death—the death of God's enemies!

Do you see how one truth logically leads to the next? Paul started with what he learned growing up, what he was taught, and how he was influenced as a child. This led to a conviction about serving God which meant hating the enemies of God and killing them. The desire to kill them became an obsession that could not be contained. It became the purpose of his life which ultimately became a celebration of death!

In Acts 7:51–8:4, we read of Paul's leadership in the murder of Stephen and the persecution of the early Christian church. Stephen was preaching the gospel to his own people—the Jewish people. Because of the corruption of that system, they had come to believe they were spiritually superior. They became proud and arrogant. They saw everybody else as the enemy. They had a legalistic sense of earning God's approval. Instead of believing in God's grace, they believed in works and earning his approval—even by killing God's enemies. Stephen was one of their own! He knew the system. Therefore, Stephen's preaching to them was intense and focused:

> You stiff-necked people! Your hearts and ears are still uncircumcised. *You are just like your ancestors*: You always resist the Holy Spirit! *Was there ever a prophet your ancestors did not persecute?* They even killed those who predicted the coming of the Righteous One. And now you have betrayed and murdered him—you who have received the law that was given through angels but have not obeyed it.

You received the truth but didn't obey it! You listened to all the perverse interpretations of it and you followed men instead of God. And the response that followed was brutal:

A TIME *for* HOPE

When the members of the Sanhedrin heard this, they were furious and gnashed their teeth at him.

We are supposed to be convicted by the Word of God — not mad at it!

But Stephen, full of the Holy Spirit, looked up to heaven and saw the glory of God, and Jesus standing at the right hand of God. "Look," he said, "I see heaven open and the Son of Man standing at the right hand of God."

At this they covered their ears and, yelling at the top of their voices, they all rushed at him, dragged him out of the city and began to stone him. Meanwhile, the witnesses *laid their coats at the feet of a young man named Saul*.

While they were stoning him, Stephen prayed, "Lord Jesus, receive my spirit." Then he fell on his knees and cried out, "Lord, do not hold this sin against them." When he had said this, he fell asleep.

And *Saul approved of their killing him*. On that day a great persecution broke out against the church in Jerusalem, and all except the apostles were scattered throughout Judea and Samaria. Godly men buried Stephen and mourned deeply for him. But *Saul began to destroy the church. Going from house to house, he dragged off both men and women and put them in prison.*

Saul's entire life was devoted to hunting down and killing God's enemies. It was an *obsession that resulted in the celebration of death*. Years later in Acts 22:4 Paul would confess to the Jewish crowd that "I persecuted the followers of this Way to their death." Later still he would confess to King Agrippa in Acts 26:10, "*When they were put to death — I cast my vote against them.*"

We will never forget the images of Muslims in major cities in America, the Middle East, Europe and Canada publically *celebrating* in the streets as they heard the news that thousands of men, women, and children had been slaughtered on 9/11!

National Geographic did a documentary on 9/11 tracking Bin Laden's terrorist highjackers. The program ended with a quote from Bin Laden as he was interviewed by an ABC journalist, "We love death...America loves life...that is the difference between us."

What a difference it makes when we worship and serve a God of love—instead of a God of hate! The Apostle John near the end of his life tells us in 1 John 3:10-16 how we can tell the difference between the children of God and the children of the devil:

> This is how we know who the children of God are and who the children of the devil are: Anyone who does not do what is right is not God's child, nor is anyone who does not love their brother and sister.

> For this is the message you heard from the beginning: **We should love one another.** Do not be like Cain, who belonged to the evil one and murdered his brother. And why did he murder him? Because his own actions were evil and his brother's were righteous. Do not be surprised, my brothers and sisters, if the world hates you. We know that we have passed from death to life, because we love each other. Anyone who does not love remains in death. Anyone who hates a brother or sister is a murderer, and you know that **no murderer has eternal life residing in him.**

> This is how we know what love is: Jesus Christ laid down his life for us. And we ought to lay down our lives for our brothers and sisters.

I am reminded of the thief on the cross. He repented and asked Jesus to "remember" him. The Lord replied with a term we hear a lot in Islam, "Today you shall be with me in **Paradise**." Islamic terrorists are encouraging young men and women to destroy their lives before they even live them! They are teaching them that this is how you serve God—by killing yourself and killing others—and promising them paradise! What an abomination! But on the cross Jesus said to the repentant thief who believed in Him, "Today you shall be with me in Paradise." (Luke 23:43) Jesus teaches Muslims, Jews and Christians alike: You don't go to Paradise by hating and killing God's enemies! You go to Paradise by believing in and loving God's Son. Jesus Christ will then strengthen you to love your neighbor as yourself.

It is interesting and instructive to observe that Zarqawi and Osama Bin Laden are not blowing themselves up! They are telling everyone else to do it, but there is no way they will put themselves in danger. They are hiding in holes. They are protecting their own lives no matter what. This is more powerful evidence of the hypocrisy and depravity of terrorism. *True leaders never ask anyone else to do what they are not willing to do themselves.*

GRACE AND FREEDOM

Fourth and finally, Paul tells us that it was only God's sovereign grace, love and power that freed him from terrorism and transformed his life. Unless human hearts and minds are changed there will always be terrorism—but God has the power to transform us by his grace. It's all about God's willingness to forgive and to make someone a new person—and God is always willing.

One powerful example is the incredible account of Saul's spiritual transformation from a religious terrorist to an apostle of love as told in Acts 9:1-19. One of the most shocking elements of Saul's conversion is that he was in the midst of a killing spree when God saved him! He was a serial terrorist when he met God!

> Meanwhile, **Saul was still breathing out murderous threats** against the Lord's disciples. He went to the high priest and asked him for letters to the synagogues in Damascus, so that if he found any there who belonged to the Way, whether men or women, he might take them as prisoners to Jerusalem. As he neared Damascus on his journey, suddenly a light from heaven

flashed around him. He fell to the ground and heard a voice say to him, "Saul, Saul, why do you persecute me?"

"Who are you, Lord?" Saul asked.

"I am Jesus, whom you are persecuting," he replied. ***Now get up and go into the city, and you will be told what you must do.***"

How amazing is that! That's sovereign grace. Saul's only hope was that God himself would intervene in a mighty, life changing way. Finally Saul could see the light and renounce the lies he had believed about his God, about himself, about his religion and about holy war. Finally he could embrace the truth about God, sin, forgiveness and new life. It says:

> The men traveling with Saul stood there speechless; they heard the sound but did not see anyone. Saul got up from the ground, but when he opened his eyes he could see nothing. So they led him by the hand into Damascus. For three days he was blind and did not eat or drink anything.

I am still convinced the reason God kept Saul physically blind for three days was to impress on him again how spiritually blind he had been for so long—even while he was convinced that he knew the truth. This is so powerful!

> In Damascus there was a disciple named Ananias. The Lord called to him in a vision, "Ananias!"

> "Yes, Lord," he answered.

> The Lord told him, "Go to the house of Judas on Straight Street and ask for a man from Tarsus named Saul, for he is praying. In a vision he has seen a man named Ananias come and place his hands on him to restore his sight."

> "Lord," Ananias answered, "I have heard many reports about this man and all the harm he has done to your holy people in Jerusalem. And he has come here with authority from the chief priests to arrest all who call on your name."

A TIME *for* HOPE

Ananias was no dummy. He knew this guy was a hit man. He was a terrorist! He was saying , "Lord—can we talk? Can we discuss this? Do I get a vote on this!" But notice what the Lord said:

> But the Lord said to Ananias, "Go! *This man is my chosen instrument* to proclaim my name to the Gentiles and their kings and to the people of Israel. I will show him how much *he must suffer for my name*."

Saul was now a trophy of God's grace. He was chosen. God had a plan for this man before he was born—before he created the world, God knew this man. God knew Saul would be a terrorist, but God also knew that he would deliver him from hate and murder. Saul would now carry the name of Jesus Christ—the name that he had maligned and blasphemed—to the Gentiles, to their kings and to the people of Israel. The terrorist was now God's ambassador of goodwill. The persecutor was now the persecuted. The hunter was now the hunted. The one who had inflicted such suffering in the name of God would now suffer for the name of God! What an awesome God! What a word from the Lord!

> Then Ananias went to the house and entered it. Placing his hands on Saul, he said, "Brother Saul, the Lord Jesus, who appeared to you on the road as you were coming here, has sent me so that you may see again and be filled with the Holy Spirit." Immediately, something like scales fell from Saul's eyes, and he could see again. He got up and was baptized, and after taking some food he regained his strength.

The most amazing evidence of Saul's conversion in the years that followed was his love for his Jewish brethren who now treated him as an enemy and an outcast and wanted him dead! In Romans 9:1-5 Paul says that if it was possible he would forfeit his own salvation in order that his Jewish brethren would be saved!

> I speak the truth in Christ—I am not lying, my conscience confirms it through the Holy Spirit—I have great sorrow and unceas-

ing anguish in my heart. *For I could wish that I myself were cursed and cut off from Christ for the sake of my people, those of my own race, the people of Israel.* Theirs is the adoption to sonship; theirs the divine glory, the covenants, the receiving of the law, the temple worship and the promises. Theirs are the patriarchs, and from them is traced the human ancestry of the Messiah, who is God over all, forever praised! Amen.

In Romans 10:1-4 Paul reveals the deepest desire of his heart for his Jewish brethren:

Brothers and sisters, *my heart's desire and prayer to God for the Israelites is that they may be saved.* For I can testify about them that they are zealous for God, but their zeal is not based on knowledge. Since they did not know the righteousness of God and sought to establish their own, they did not submit to God's righteousness. Christ is the culmination of the law so that there may be righteousness for everyone who believes.

In Romans 11:1-6 Paul rejoices in the truth that there is a remnant of the Jewish people who will be redeemed by the grace and love of God:

I ask then: Did God reject his people? By no means! I am an Israelite myself, a descendant of Abraham, from the tribe of Benjamin. God did not reject his people, whom he fore-knew. Don't you know what Scripture says in the passage about Elijah—how he appealed to God against Israel: "Lord, they have killed your prophets and torn down your altars; I am the only one left, and they are trying to kill me?" And what was God's answer to him? "I have reserved for myself seven thousand who have not bowed the knee to Baal." So too, *at the present time there is a remnant chosen by grace.* And if by grace, then it cannot be based on works; if it were, grace would no longer be grace.

A Time *for* Hope

Paul tells us again that it was only God's sovereign grace, love and power that freed him from a life of terrorism and delivered him to a life of love. The cure for terrorism is the gospel of Jesus Christ.

In the name of God the Father and God the Son and God the Holy Spirit. Amen.

PART III

A Biblical Look at Islam

CHAPTER 6
*The Biblical God **I AM** or Allah*

A BIBLICAL LOOK AT ISLAM

SUNDAY, OCTOBER 28, 2001

To understand 9/11, we must understand two things: Not every Muslim is a terrorist, but every 9/11 terrorist was a Muslim. These 19 men were all inspired and empowered by their God, their prophet, their holy book, and their religion.

These are difficult times to have an open and honest discussion and dialogue about truth, and about competing world views and religions. Naturally, we all want to be sensitive to others and to show love. Nevertheless, the fact remains that it is only truth that sets people free. It is only truth that transforms people, nations, and the world! We must love our neighbor, even as we ask certain vital questions: Where is God? Who is God? Who can help us find God? How can we follow God? These are fundamental questions. When we, as Christians, sing genuinely from our hearts "Alleluia, praise the Lord"—are we worshipping the same God that our Muslim friends and neighbors worship when they shout out genuinely "Allahu Akbar—God is great"? Many insist that we are worshipping the same God, simply calling him by a different name. I think the world community longs for the answer to be "Yes". However, it's not global longing or personal opinion that provides an accurate and authoritative answer. If Christians worship the same God as Muslims, then we need to ask another question: Why do Islam and Christianity have such different and at times contradictory concepts of God? For instance, why do Christianity and Islam have opposite views of the supremacy of Jesus and Mohammad? What about the issue of the Bible or the Koran being the ultimate and final written revelation of God? What about the different views of salvation? What about God's nature, character and personality? What about how we receive forgiveness, hope and a future?

One politically incorrect answer to these questions is that Christians and Muslims do not worship the same God—and I believe this response is a biblical one. The Scriptures clearly teach that God has revealed himself in the Messiah, Jesus Christ, and that he is the only hope for Muslims, Christians, Jews, Agnostics, Atheists and everyone else. I don't say this to condemn Muslims. Most of them absolutely agree that they don't worship the same God as Christians! This is not about condemnation, but about believing that Jesus Christ is the only hope the human race has in order to know God personally and to live in peace with one another.

9/11 tragically has provided a teachable moment—therefore we will consider Islam in light of the Bible. The world is ignorant of and confused about Islam. President Bush himself, who is doing a great job dealing with the emergency terrorism situation, showed some of the confusion that we all have about Islam. In a powerful speech that he gave to Congress, which was one of the greatest speeches I have ever heard, while rightly calling for love and respect between people of different faiths, said, "By the way, Islam means peace." It's true that the word *Islam* is related to the Arabic word *salam* which means peace, but Islam does not mean peace. The word means *submission*. A Muslim is one who submits his will to the sovereign will of Allah and his prophet Mohammad. It is vitally important to understand that history is witness to the bitter truth that Islam also forces others to submit to Allah. Islam is known as the religion of the sword. When we speak of Islam, we speak of the sword of Islam. I am not saying that every Muslim is a terrorist—of course not! A majority of Muslims want peace. They are our friends, co-workers, neighbors and fellow American patriots. Nevertheless, Islam throughout history has expanded by war and by the sword. These expansions were led by Muslims who became terrorists! And we continue to see this today in Indonesia, the Philippines, the Sudan, Afghanistan, and now we have seen this same terror in New York City.

Islam is a sensitive yet necessary topic to address. As we evaluate Islam in the light of Scripture, it is not my desire to preach Islam, Allah or Mohammad—I preach Christ. However, I believe that as Christians we need to understand Islam in order to have a more effective witness to Muslims. As we compare Islam and Christianity, we will also grow in our thanksgiving to God for the grace that he has given us in Jesus Christ.

Islam began around 610 AD when a man from Arabia named Mohammad claimed to have received revelations from God mediated through the angel Gabriel. Islam teaches that for a period of about 20 years Mohammad received these amazing divine revelations. The best way to evaluate Islam is to compare the claims of Mohammad to the teaching of Scripture to find out if Christians and Muslims really do worship the same God. The most important revelation that Mohammad claimed to receive, which is the foundation of Islam, states: *there is no God but Allah and Mohammad is his prophet.* This is the first revelation that Mohammad says he received. When you read the Koran—and I encourage you to read it in order to better understand Islam—you find that it is divided into 114 chapters called surahs. They are ordered from the longest to the shortest and every chapter begins this way: "In the name of Allah, the compassionate, the merciful." Every chapter begins this way because Mohammad said that there is only one God and his name is Allah. The name Allah means *the God* in Arabic.

As we begin to evaluate this claim biblically, it's interesting to note that two thousand years before Mohammad claimed to have received the revelation of God's name, Moses, a man highly respected by Islam, had a dramatic encounter with the living God. The encounter, which took place around 1500 BC, is described in Exodus 3. What is so fascinating is the element of time. From Mohammad's day (AD 600) back to Moses is 2100 years. From our day back to Mohammad is 1400 years. There is a much greater time lapse between Moses and Mohammad than between Mohammad and us! Islam has a major burden to try to explain the revelation of God's name to Moses two millennia before Mohammad.

> Now Moses was tending the flock of Jethro his father-in-law, the priest of Midian, and he led the flock to the far side of the wilderness and came to Horeb, the mountain of God. There the angel of the LORD appeared to him in flames of fire from within a bush. Moses saw that though the bush was on fire it did not burn up. (Exodus 3:1-2)

When you study the Scriptures you find that when the angel of the Lord is mentioned in a particular way—with the definite article *the angel of the Lord*—this always refers to a theophany, an appearance of God Himself; and specifically to a pre-incarnate appearance of the second member of the Godhead—the eternal Logos, Jesus Christ. Notice what follows:

> So Moses thought, "I will go over and see this strange sight— why the bush does not burn up." When the LORD saw that he had gone over to look, God called to him from within the bush, "Moses! Moses!"

> And Moses said, "Here I am."

> "Do not come any closer," God said. "Take off your sandals, for the place where you are standing is holy ground." Then he said, "I am the God of your father the God of Abraham, the God of Isaac and the God of Jacob." At this, Moses hid his face, because he was afraid to look at God. The LORD said, "I have indeed seen the misery of my people in Egypt. I have heard them crying out because of their slave drivers, and I am concerned about their suffering. So I have come down to rescue them..." (Exodus 3:3-7)

Our Muslim friends respect Moses—they consider him one of their prophets. When you read the Koran and consider the attributes of Allah, you find that Allah is a distant, impersonal and inscrutable God. He cannot be known. Muslim scholars acknowledge this truth. All that can be known about Allah is his will revealed through Mohammad and the Koran, because Allah himself is an impersonal God. Now when you understand this about Allah, and you read in Exodus 3 that God says, "I have heard them crying because of their slave drivers; I am concerned about their suffering and I have come down to rescue them" —you realize that the God of Exodus 3 is not the God of Islam. This is the God of the Old and New Testament who ultimately reveals himself in the Messiah, Jesus Christ—the God who is on a rescue mission.

> So I have come down to rescue them from the hand of the Egyptians and to bring them up out of that land into a good and spacious land, a land flowing with milk and honey—the home of the Canaanites, Hittites, Amorites, Perizzites, Hivites and Jebusites. And now the cry of the Israelites has reached me, and I have seen the way the Egyptians are oppressing them. So now, go. I am sending you to Pharaoh to bring my people the Israelites out of Egypt. (Exodus 3:8-10)

This God is transcendent, but also the God who cares about us. He is the God who is with us. He is the God who can be known by us. This God can be approached and appealed to. He is a very different God from Allah.

Then Moses says what all of us would have said:

> "Who am I that I should go to Pharaoh and bring the Israelites out of Egypt?" And God said, "I will be with you. And this will be the sign to you that it is I who have sent you: When you have brought the people out of Egypt, you will worship God on this mountain."

> Moses said to God, "Suppose I go to the Israelites and say to them, 'The God of your fathers has sent me to you,' and they ask me, 'What is his name?' Then what shall I tell them?"

A Time *for* Hope

God said to Moses, "I AM WHO I AM." This is what you are to say to the Israelites: "I AM has sent me to you." (Exodus 3:11-14)

Two thousand years before Mohammad, God revealed to Moses, a man revered as a prophet by Islam, that his name was *I AM WHO I AM.* His name was and is and always will be the eternal, the self-existent one—*I AM.*

God also said to Moses, Say to the Israelites, "The LORD, the God of your fathers—the God of Abraham, the God of Isaac and the God of Jacob—has sent me to you." (Exodus 3:15)

God named himself *the LORD.* This name *LORD,* in English capital letters, represents the four Hebrew consonants that became known as the four letters—the Tetragrammaton—the sacred name. This name was so holy that the Jews wouldn't even speak it out loud. God said, "You go tell them that *this one*, the one with the sacred name—*I AM* has sent you." And notice:

This is my name forever, the name you shall call me from generation to generation. (Exodus 3:15)

When did God change his name? And the answer is—he never did. So why does Mohammad, 2100 years after the fact, say that God told him that his name is Allah?

It's very interesting to note that when you go back in time 500 years from Moses to Abraham, who is highly revered by Islam, you find that Abraham also knew this God whose name is *I AM.* Abraham would become the father of the Jewish people through Isaac and Jacob, and the father of the Arab people through Ishmael. So Abraham, the father of the Jews and the Arabs worshipped and obeyed *I AM WHO I AM.*

After this, the word of *the LORD* came to Abram in a vision: "Do not be afraid, Abram. I am your shield, your very great reward." (Genesis 15:1)

God promises that he will establish his covenant with Abraham, and later affirms that covenant with Isaac and Jacob. Therefore, we read in Genesis 15:17:

When the sun had set and darkness had fallen, a smoking firepot with a blazing torch appeared and passed between the pieces. On that day *the LORD* made a covenant with Abram and said, "To your descendants I give this land, from the Wadi of Egypt to the great river, the Euphrates..." (Genesis 15:17-18)

You see, in verse 18, it is *the LORD* — the four letters, the sacred name, *I AM WHO I* AM — that establishes his covenant with Abraham. It is this God, with this name, who makes this promise to Abraham and his descendents — the Jews.

You may say, "Well, Pastor Dave does that mean God doesn't love anybody but the Jews?" Far from it — just the opposite is true. In Genesis 16 we read of Hagar, an Egyptian woman, who also knew the God who is *I AM WHO I AM*. Hagar is the slave woman that Abraham used and abused in an effort to receive the promise of God through ungodly means. Instead of trusting God to fulfill his promise his way, Abraham took Hagar at his wife Sarah's invitation, and exploited her for his own purposes, and then cast her off. But God didn't forget her. God didn't turn his back on her:

The angel of *the LORD* found Hagar near a spring in the desert; it was the spring that is beside the road to Shur. And he said, "Hagar, slave of Sarai, where have you come from, and where are you going?"

"I'm running away from my mistress Sarai," she answered. (Genesis 16:7-8)

It is the Angel of the Lord who finds her. This is the same Angel of the Lord who revealed himself to Moses as the God of Abraham, Isaac, and Jacob in Exodus 3. This is the living, eternal, transcendent and personal God who reveals himself in Jesus Christ. And this God loves Abraham and Moses — and he also loves Hagar, an Egyptian woman, and her son Ishmael who had been thrown away and left to die:

A Time *for* Hope

Then the angel of *the LORD* told her, "Go back to your mistress and submit to her." The angel added, "I will increase your descendants so much that they will be too numerous to count." (Exodus 16:9-10)

The Lord who is the great I AM promised her that as she obeyed and served him, and was willing to go back and submit to her master and mistress, that God would fulfill his great plans for her and her son:

The angel of *the LORD* also said to her: "You are now pregnant and you will give birth to a son. You shall name him Ishmael, for *the LORD* has heard of your misery." (Exodus 16:11)

This God is not a distant, impersonal God, like Allah. This God is close by, knowable, and relates to us personally—not just clinically, by decree and fate. He loves us and calls us by name. And God, while loving the Arab people, is also up front about what their future holds. In speaking of Ishmael, God says:

He will be a wild donkey of a man; his hand will be against everyone and everyone's hand against him, and he will live in hostility toward all his brothers. (Exodus 16:12)

God prophesies that the nations and tribes that will come from Ishmael will be greatly blessed by him, but they will also cause much trouble for each other and be in conflict with everyone else all the time.

God's love for Hagar impacted her deeply:

She gave this name to *the LORD* who spoke to her: "You are the God who sees me," for she said, "I have now seen the One who sees me." (Genesis 16:13)

Hagar knew the God that Abraham knew and the God that Moses would know 500 years later, whose name was not Allah—his name was *I AM WHO I AM*. We don't know exactly how his name was pronounced because the Jews didn't speak his name and their writings didn't have vowels. No one knows which vowels went with the four consonants in God's name. I have a feeling that's exactly the way God wanted it to be! Nevertheless, we know his name is *I AM WHO I AM.* "You go and tell them—*I AM* sent you to them," said The LORD.

Hagar knew this one true God; Ishmael her son knew him also. In Genesis 17:15, after God had given Abraham Ishmael, God promised Abraham a son through Sarah. This son would be the son of the covenant:

> God also said to Abraham, "As for Sarai your wife, you are no longer to call her Sarai; her name will be Sarah. I will bless her and will surely give you a son by her. I will bless her so that she will be the mother of nations; kings of peoples will come from her." (Genesis 17:15-16)

When Abraham heard this, he did what any of us would have done at 100 years of age...he laughed:

> Abraham fell face down; he laughed and said to himself, "Will a son be born to a man a hundred years old? Will Sarah bear a child at the age of ninety?" And Abraham said to God, "If only Ishmael might live under your blessing!" (Genesis 17:17-18)

Abraham seems to be saying: God, you have already given me Ishmael, and I think that's about the only miracle I am capable of, so let's just work with Ishmael. I'm not sure Lord that we can have another one:

> Then God said, "Yes, but your wife Sarah will bear you a son, and you will call him Isaac (*meaning laughter*), I will establish my covenant with him as an everlasting covenant for his descendants after him." (Genesis 17:19)

God was saying unequivocally that he would establish his covenant with Isaac and his descendants, the Jewish people, through whom the Messiah, Jesus Christ, would come:

> And as for Ishmael, "I have heard you..." (Genesis 17:20)

A TIME *for* HOPE

But God loves the Arabs (the descendants of Ishmael) too! Abraham is Ishmael's father, and he cares for him. Ishmael is not the son of the covenant, but he is loved by Abraham, his earthly father, and by his heavenly Father also:

> I will surely bless him; I will make him fruitful and will greatly increase his numbers. He will be the father of twelve rulers, and I will make him into a great nation—but my covenant I will establish with Isaac. (Genesis 17:20-21)

If you know and love history as I do, you understand that in the *Dark Ages*, while Christian Europe deteriorated spiritually, morally, intellectually and culturally—Islamic civilization flourished in science, medicine, literature and philosophy. God made the Arabs a great people, but it was *I AM WHO I AM* who kept his promise to bless them—not Allah. Hagar knew the God *I AM,* and so did Ishmael—who would become the father of the Arab nations.

In the book of Genesis we read:

> This is the account of the family line of Abraham's son Ishmael, whom Sarah's slave, Hagar the Egyptian, bore to Abraham. These are the names of the sons of Ishmael, listed in the order of their birth: Nebaioth the firstborn of Ishmael, Kedar, Adbeel, Mibsam, Mishma, Dumah, Massa, Hadad, Tema, Jetur, Naphish and Kedemah. These were the sons of Ishmael, and these are the names of the twelve tribal rulers according to their settlements and camps. Ishmael lived a hundred and thirty-seven years. He breathed his last and died, and he was gathered to his people. His descendants settled in the area from Havilah to Shur, near the eastern border of Egypt, as you go toward Ashur. (Genesis 25:12-18)

The Bible mentions their names and the places they settled and the fact that God blessed the Arabs also—just as he promised.

In Genesis 21, we have the story of how Abraham and Sarah had cast Hagar and Ishmael out a second time. Ishmael was a teenager at that point, and was dying of thirst in the wilderness with Hagar nearby:

> Early the next morning Abraham took some food and a skin of water and gave them to Hagar. He set them on her shoulders and then sent her off with the boy. She went on her way and wandered in the Desert of Beersheba.

> When the water in the skin was gone, she put the boy under one of the bushes. Then she went off and sat down about a bowshot away, for she thought, "I cannot watch the boy die." (Genesis 21:14-16)

Do you think God didn't know her tragic situation? That he didn't care? That he didn't love her by name?

> And as she sat there, she began to sob. God heard the boy crying, and the angel of God called to Hagar from heaven... (Genesis 21:16-17)

This is the God who actually sees us and hears us. This is the God who is high and lifted up and also right here—Immanuel, God is with us. This is the God who never changes but also the God who can be appealed to. This is the one true God—*I AM WHO I AM:*

> God called to Hagar from heaven and said to her, "What is the matter, Hagar? Do not be afraid; God has heard the boy crying as he lies there." (Genesis 21:17)

Does God really care about a boy who is not the child of the covenant? Does he really care about an Egyptian woman—a single mom—a slave?

> "Lift the boy up and take him by the hand, for I will make him into a great nation." Then God opened her eyes and she saw a well of water. So she went and filled the skin with water and

gave the boy a drink. *God was with the boy as he grew up.* (Genesis 21:18-20)

God was with Abraham's son, Ishmael, who became the father of the Arab nations. Ishmael, a forefather of Mohammad, knew and worshipped the great *I AM*! How tragically sad it is, however, that over the next 2500 years, even as the Jewish people (the Israelites) dishonored God by their idolatry, so did the descendants of Abraham through Ishmael, the Arab. They did not remain faithful to the God of Hagar and Ishmael—the God of the Old Testament—the great *I AM THAT I AM.*

Saudi Arabia and the cities of Mecca and Medina were rampant with idolatry and polytheism. Mohammad maintained that God had sent him to fix this situation so that the people would no longer worship idols but worship the one true God whose name, according to Mohammad, was Allah. Allah was already known in pre-Islamic Arabia and was one of the gods who was worshipped at Mecca. He was a high god, a special god and was identified as the moon god. People were encouraged to worship the god of the moon. Mohammad, in the revelation he claimed to receive, said that the moon god, Allah, was now to be worshipped as the only God.

Based on my understanding of Christianity and Islam, there are major distinctions and many outright contradictions between the God of the Bible and Allah. I do not believe that the great *I AM* of the Old and New Testament is the same God as Allah of Islam. They are different Gods, with a different name, a different nature and character, a different covenant, a different holy book, a different purpose and agenda, a different moral code, a different way of salvation, and a different chief prophet and apostle. Other than that, they are identical!

I know how the world longs for unity—we all do. So I know how the world longs to say, "Look—the Jews, the Christians, and the Muslims all worship one God. They just call him by a different name. But he's the same God for all of them—that's why we refer to them as the three great monotheistic faiths."

And there is some truth to all of this. All these three great religions worship one God. And by "great religions" I mean influential in the sense that each one has had a huge impact on the human race and history. But sometimes what people don't understand is—you can worship one God and still worship a different God than someone else who worships one God! When you look closely at the God of the Bible and the God of Islam, it is shockingly clear that they are not the same God! So much for our politically correct comfort zone!

When Mohammad said there is no God but Allah, he also claimed that he, Mohammad, was the prophet of God—the last prophet, the greatest prophet. If Mohammad is the last and greatest prophet and apostle of God, then God has been revealing himself progressively and has given his final revelation through Islam. This means Islam is the only true faith. But if Jesus is the last and greatest prophet of God, the Son of God, the author and finisher of our faith—then Mohammad, whether knowingly or unknowingly, intentionally or unintentionally, is a fraud and Islam is a lie. Everybody comfortable?

In the name of God the Father and God the Son and God the Holy Spirit. Amen.

AUTHOR'S NOTE:

In the March 6, 2010 edition of the *Wall Street Journal*, in the Weekend Interview, Matthew Kaminski spoke with Mosab Yousef, the author of *Son of Hamas,* whose father is a Hamas leader imprisoned in the West Bank. Kaminski asked Mr. Yousef:

"Do you consider your father a fanatic?"

"He's not a fanatic," says Mr. Yousef. "He's a very moderate, logical person. What matters is not whether my father is a fanatic or not—he's doing the will of a fanatic God. It doesn't matter if he's a terrorist or a traditional Muslim. At the end of the day a traditional Muslim is doing the will of a fanatic, fundamentalist, terrorist God. I know this is harsh to say. Most governments avoid this subject. They don't want to admit this is an ideological war."

"The problem is not in Muslims," he continues. "The problem is with their God. They need to be liberated from their God. He is their biggest enemy. It has been 1,400 years they have been lied to."

In May of 2010 in New York City, I had the privilege of hearing Mosab Yousef in person. Mosab has become a believer in Jesus Christ and is now sharing his faith, hoping to be an instrument in bringing peace between the Israelis and the Palestinians. In his message in New York City, he made a number of comments about the God of Islam — all of which powerfully illustrate that the God of the Bible is not the God of Islam. Mosab said the following:

1. When interacting with Muslims, don't make it a religious war — Muslims against Christians. Make it an ideological war: Christianity's God of love vs. Islam's God of hate.

2. Allah hates the Jews. The Koran refers to them as the offspring of pigs and monkeys. Because they occupied Palestinian land and tortured me personally, I also hated the Jews and wanted to kill them to serve Allah.

3. The value system of the Middle East is based upon shame and honor — not right and wrong. As a Muslim I also had to deal with Allah, who is the God of shame, guilt and fear. The answer to Allah is the (Christian) God of grace, love and freedom.

4. (Islamic) Terrorists are deceived. They are the victims of their own God. The problem is not Muslims, but Islam. The problem is Islam's ideology, God, prophet, and book.

5. If Muslims follow the example of Mohammad—they will all be terrorists!

Christians and Muslims do not worship the same God! As you can imagine, Mosab Yousef's life is now threatened on a regular basis. This courageous young man continues to trust God and serve as an instrument of his peace and reconciliation.

CHAPTER 7
Jesus or Mohammad

A BIBLICAL LOOK AT ISLAM

SUNDAY, NOVEMBER 4, 2001

Osama Bin Laden, in his most recent communication to the world, made a very succinct and terrifying statement: "True Muslims every-where celebrated the attacks of September 11th." Now I personally believe that most Muslims are peaceful and they don't celebrate hate and murder. The majority of Muslims are not terrorists in any way, but the terrorists of September 11th were all Muslims—and that's important to know. It means that at least for them, their commitment to Islam, to Allah, to Mohammad and the Koran was the decisive factor in the terror they perpetrated. That's a fact. They would tell you the same thing. Just because most Muslims are peace loving does not mean that Islam by nature is a religion of peace. It is vital to understand this. The verdict of history is clear: Islam is not a religion of peace, and Mohammad was not a man of peace.

The renowned historian, Will Durant, who was not a religious apolo-gist but a secularist, gave some powerful historical insights into the history of Mohammad and Islam. In his influential magnum opus, *The Story of Civilization* (Volume 4, *The Age of Faith*), he traces the growth of Judaism, Christianity and Islam from 300 AD to 1300 AD. In Chapter 8, entitled *Mohammad*, Durant and other historians as well come to some very interesting conclusions concerning Islam and Mohammad. First, Islam in its first hundred years grew and expanded through one method and one means—war, military conquest and jihad. Secondly, Mohammad led his own army into battle dozens of times and was wounded seriously on a couple of occasions. Mohammad was a man of war. He killed people in battle. He also led his army in caravan raids in which people were kidnapped and held for ransom. Mohammad in Surah 47:4 of the Koran, entitled *Mohammad,* says:

> So, when you clash with the unbelievers, smite their necks until
> you overpower them. Then hold them in bondage, then either
> free them graciously, or free them after taking a ransom, until
> war shall come to an end.

These are Mohammad's own words. It's interesting that the Taliban today in Afghanistan does the exact same thing. They continue to hear Mohammad say, "Smite their necks, take them captive and hold them for ransom until the war is over." As a matter of fact, the Taliban took two young women, Heather and Dana, captive a couple of months ago and they are holding them for ransom. It's all over the news. The ransom being—if the United States does not attack Afghanistan they will release those two young ladies. The Taliban are imitating Mohammad. They are not only hearing his words, they are following his violent example.

Mohammad also, along with his army, forced people to convert to Islam under the threat of death—this is historical fact. Mohammad practiced revenge killing against his personal enemies. He literally took hits out on them and had them murdered. Mohammad and his army also sold women and children into slavery after killing the men in battle. The Islamic military in northern Sudan is doing exactly the same thing today. They are killing the Christian men in the south of Sudan and taking the women and children captive, abusing them, and holding them for ransom—exactly like Mohammad their prophet.

Now, some may object and say, 'Well, Pastor Dave, that's true, but throughout history Christian people, organizations and nations have also engaged in terrorism, war and murder." And you know what—that's true. Sometimes people and nations, who identify with Christ, have done horrible things. But I want you to be aware of the one critical, profound difference—whenever a Christian individual or nation engages in terrorism it is always in direct contradiction of and opposition to Jesus Christ's own personal teaching and example. When Islamic terrorists participate in such actions, their actions are consistent with the teaching and the example of Mohammad. Which prophet would you rather trust with your life? With your family? With your world?

Even though most Muslims rightly repudiate hatred, murder and terror—sadly, Islam, when viewed historically and objectively, does not repudiate such actions. It never has.

It is important to compare and contrast Jesus and Mohammad. When you consider the life and teaching of Jesus with the historical record of Mohammad the contrast could not be more shocking and thought provoking. Jesus said in Matthew 5:43 to his followers:

> You have heard that it was said, "Love your neighbor and hate your enemy." But I tell you, "love your enemies and pray for those who persecute you..." (Matthew 5:43-44)

That is the heart and mind of Jesus—this is not the heart and mind of Mohammad. These are the words of Jesus—they are definitely not the words of Mohammad. Jesus continues:

> ...that you may be children of your Father in heaven. He causes his sun to rise on the evil and the good, and sends rain on the righteous and the unrighteous. If you love those who love you, what reward will you get? Are not even the tax collectors doing that? And if you greet only your own people, what are you doing more than others? Do not even pagans do that? Be perfect, therefore, as your heavenly Father is perfect. (Matthew 5:44-48)

A TIME *for* HOPE

What kind of world do you want for yourself, for your wife and children, for your friends and neighbors? Be careful to what prophet you give your allegiance!

Jesus said "Love your enemies—pray for those who persecute you." That's my kind of prophet!

Matthew 26 describes the night before the crucifixion as Jesus is betrayed by Judas and arrested. Jesus says to Judas:

> "Do what you came for, friend." Then the men stepped forward, seized Jesus and arrested him. With that, one of Jesus' companions (*Peter*) reached for his sword, drew it out and struck the servant of the high priest, cutting off his ear. (Matthew 26:50-51)

That could have been the beginning of the sword of Christianity right there—but it wasn't—because of the leadership of Jesus! This is in contrast to Islam, which 600 years later became the religion of the sword because of the leadership of Mohammad—and it still is today, evidenced by the terror of 9/11. Notice Jesus' response to Peter:

> "Put your sword back in its place," Jesus said to him, "for all who draw the sword will die by the sword." (Matthew 26:52)

Jesus says—I'm a loving prophet, I'm the merciful Savior. I come to establish peace, to bring hope, to bring forgiveness, to reconcile enemies. I don't come to start jihad against the enemies of Christianity. This is the Christ that we follow. This is the Christ that our Muslims friends need to know. The Christ who is the embodiment of God, the one who is high and lifted up—the transcendent one—yes—but also the God who is personal and imminent—the God who is with us—Immanuel. The knowable God! Our Muslim friends believe in a God who is unknowable, distant and impersonal. They believe that the only thing they can know about their God is his will—they can never know him. The one they need to know is Jesus the Messiah, the Son of the living God.

Luke 9:51 is the fulfillment of Isaiah 50:7, written 700 years earlier, which said that the Messiah was going to *set his face like flint* and go to the cross as the suffering servant of God:

> As the time approached for him to be taken up to heaven, Jesus resolutely set out for Jerusalem. And he sent messengers on ahead, who went into a Samaritan village to get things ready for him... (Luke 9:51-52)

The Samaritans were considered inferior by their Jewish cousins. They were scorned as half breeds and considered defective spiritually, racially and ethnically. The Jews considered them to be the *untouchables* of their day. Jesus was heading for Jerusalem and he had a plan:

> ...but the people there did not welcome him, because he was heading for Jerusalem. When the disciples James and John saw this, they asked, "Lord, do you want us to call fire down from heaven to destroy them?" (Matthew 9:53-54)

It was as if they were asking Jesus—Lord if they are not willing to convert and believe in you should we just destroy them? But Jesus turned and rebuked them and said:

> You do not know what manner of spirit you are of. For the Son of Man did not come to destroy men's lives but to save them. (Luke 9:55-56 NKJ)

Do you think the outcome for the Samaritan village would have been different if it was Mohammad and his army that had shown up? It was Jesus who protected the lives of the people in Samaria—that's the Messiah we follow. That's the prophet we follow. That's the God we worship. That is why we say unapologetically, yet lovingly: the God of Islam is not the God of Christianity. Our Muslim friends need to know the great God who is the *I AM WHO I AM* of the Old Testament and the Father, Son and Holy Spirit of the New Testament.

A Time *for* Hope

Jesus is the Christ and the prophet who has come—greater than Moses and greater than Mohammad! This is the Savior who sets the captives free.

We have been getting hundreds of letters in response to our radio ministry after 9/11. I could never share them all, but let me share a few:

> The protestant community at Bedford Hills Correctional Facility would like to receive the free series on Ground Zero and the hope that we have. The women here appreciate the gospel made available through your station.

It was the Protestant chaplain who asked us to send all the tapes because so many of the ladies in prison want to hear the gospel. Jesus is the prophet who sets them free:

> I was listening to my radio in my cell here at Sing Sing Correctional Facility. I was moved by the ministry of the good news and the ministry of hope. When you mentioned how your youth group and their youth pastor went out and did a *prayer walk* and prayed for the city and for those who were missing, and they prayed for the families of those whose pictures had been put up on the walls, who were missing at the World Trade Center, my heart was moved by God in Jesus Christ.

This is the God who enters into our pain. This is the God who is in solidarity with the human race. This is the God who knows the territory of suffering. This is the God who reveals himself in Jesus Christ—"a man of sorrows, and acquainted with grief." (Isaiah 53:3)

> Dear Calvary Baptist, I am a prisoner within the New Jersey State system. Could you send me the tapes? I want to be a witness in prison for the Lord.

> Dear Calvary and Pastor Dave, I have been listening to your radio program for some time now. It's been a big inspiration to me. The Lord Jesus saved me from my sins through listening to you every morning and some nights. I would like to come to New York now and fellowship with you one day...I love hear-

ing you and Calvary share the gospel. May God continue to bless you. My sixteen year old daughter and I have been truly blessed as we listen together to the word of God.

And the letters go on and on—hundreds, thousands of letters. Mohammad can't do that! Only Jesus Christ can do that...only Jesus can set the captives free.

When we evaluate Islam from a biblical perspective, we are not condemning our Muslim friends and neighbors. They are just like many of us were for a long time—in spiritual darkness. Muslims follow a prophet who was a sinner like you and me. Mohammad needed God's forgiveness and grace just like you and me. I don't want to follow a sinner—I already have enough trouble! I want to follow someone who can get the job done. I want a God who can forgive me, empower me, transform me, fill me with love and peace, and give me hope and a future. Allah and Mohammad cannot do that—but Jesus Christ can.

It's not by chance that some of the most violent persecution of Christians today is done in the name of Allah, by Islamic terrorists and governments. When you consider the history of Mohammad and Islam, what is happening today around the world should not surprise you.

The *Voice of the Martyrs* is a powerful ministry of God's grace, power and compassion. In their world calendar for 2001, 6 months is consumed with Muslim persecution of Christians around the world! The following are but a few examples of such persecution:

JANUARY 2001

Nigeria and Sudan are two nations where lines of conflict exist between the mostly Muslim north and the mostly Christian south. In some Nigerian states Sharia Law has been enacted requiring all of society to live by the Q'uran—forced conversion and forced obedience. In the Sudan the Muslim government of the north has incited a jihad—a holy war against the south—killing or enslaving all who refuse to follow Islam.

A Time *for* Hope

But despite such harsh realities the body of Christ is growing and singing praises to the one who sits on the throne.

MAY 2001

A majority of the Christians in Iran are of Armenian descent, therefore pastors have been warned by the militant Islamic government that they can only preach in Armenian in order to prevent further converts among the Farsi speaking people who primarily follow Islam. However, because of the hope that is in them, some pastors in Iran ignore this order and take great risks to preach in Farsi, converting Muslims who are then persecuted by their family.

JULY 2001

In July, the Arabic speaking nations of the world bend their knee to Allah, the God of the Muslims. One of the most difficult groups of people to reach for Christ is the Muslim community. Muslims who convert to Christ in many Arab speaking nations face serious opposition from friends and family. Some are even killed.

In the January 2004 issue of *Voice of the Martyrs magazine*, an article entitled *Radical Islam, No Stranger to Our Family,* tells of the genocide of Christians in Southern Sudan, due to Islamic jihad. This is happening today, but that's also what Mohammad did 1400 years ago.

In Indonesia, there are church burnings, forced conversions and female genital mutilations. In Pakistan, there is the archaic blasphemy law and persecution of Christians. It's not by accident that some of the most brutal persecution of Christians is by Islam. It is not by chance that some of the most heinous practitioners of state supported terrorism in the world today are found in Muslim nations such as Indonesia, Sudan, Iraq, Libya, Iran, Pakistan, Syria, and the PLO and Arafat in Israel.

How do we explain all these terrible realities? Why does God allow horrible things to happen to his people including persecution by Islamic terrorism? In Matthew 5:10 Jesus helps us understand:

> Blessed are those who are persecuted because of ***righteousness***, for theirs is the kingdom of heaven. Blessed are you when people insult you, persecute you and falsely say all kinds of evil against you because of me. Rejoice and be glad, because great is your reward in heaven, for in the same way they persecuted the prophets who were before you. (Matthew 5:10-12)

Jesus says there is a blessing that attends persecution and suffering—a blessing which transcends our present circumstances. Many brothers and sisters in New York City have found that to be true in recent weeks.

Righteousness is a ***who*** not a ***what***. The Lord says that suffering and persecution is part of the way he builds true joy, peace and assurance into lives. Notice the paradoxical truth that persecution for Christ brings blessing! Only God's mind is big enough to get all the way around that one.

In John 15 the context is the upper room discourse, the night before Jesus was crucified. Jesus is sharing some great truths with his disciples before he physically leaves them and sends the Holy Spirit to live within them. He tells them:

> If the world hates you, keep in mind that it hated me first. If you belonged to the world, it would love you as its own. As it is, you do not belong to the world, but I have chosen you out of the world. That is why the world hates you. Remember what I told you: "A servant is not greater than his master. If they persecuted me, they will persecute you also. If they obeyed my teaching, they will obey yours also. They will treat you this way because of my name, for they do not know the one who sent me." (John 15:18-21)

It's important to understand that Jesus consistently taught that anyone who rejects him also rejects God the Father who sent him. He also says because the world hates him that it will also hate us. There will be times when *Christ in us* will be an offense to others—but God forbid that we should be an offense because of our unloving behavior, ungodly lifestyle, hypocrisy, brutality, injustice, insensitivity or selfishness. You and I must check our own hearts today as followers of Jesus Christ.

Let me close by telling you about the night I saw Steve Green in concert. I love Steve Green. What a gift God has given him. I love his heart, his consistent witness and the fact that he is a man of God. In the middle of his incredible concert he said, "Let me share with you a couple scriptures that are near and dear to my heart." And then he quoted by memory, with feeling, the entire chapter of Hebrews 11. We loved it—the only thing better than his singing was the way he quoted scripture.

We read in Hebrews 11:32:

> And what more shall I say? I do not have time to tell about Gideon, Barak, Samson and Jephthah, about David and Samuel and the prophets, who through faith conquered kingdoms, administered justice, and gained what was promised; who shut the mouths of lions, quenched the fury of the flames, and escaped the edge of the sword; whose weakness was turned to strength; and who became powerful in battle and routed foreign armies. Women received back their dead, raised to life again. (Hebrews 11:32-35)

Wow—what victory! So everybody had that victory? No, look at the rest of verse 35:

> There were others who were tortured, refusing to be released so that they might gain an even better resurrection. (Hebrews 11:35)

Many of our brothers and sisters in Christ are facing brutal persecution today at the hands of Islamic terrorists.

> Some faced jeers and flogging, and even chains and imprisonment. They were put to death by stoning; they were sawed in two; they were killed by the sword. They went about in sheep-

skins and goatskins, destitute, persecuted and mistreated— *the world was not worthy of them*. (Hebrews 11:36-37)

What an awesome truth—"the world was not worthy of them." And then we read verse 38 which sounds like Afghanistan today:

They wandered in deserts and mountains, living in caves and in holes in the ground. These were all commended for their faith, yet none of them received what had been promised, since God had planned something better for us so that only together with us would they be made perfect.

Therefore, since we are surrounded by such a great cloud of witnesses, let us throw off everything that hinders and the sin that so easily entangles. And let us run with perseverance the race marked out for us, fixing our eyes on Jesus, the pioneer and perfecter of faith. For the joy set before him he endured the cross, scorning its shame, and sat down at the right hand of the throne of God. Consider him who endured such opposition from sinners, so that you will not grow weary and lose heart. In your struggle against sin, you have not yet resisted to the point of shedding your blood. (Hebrews 11:38-40; 12:1-4)

God calls us to our own marathon by the grace of God. Jesus is the only way—and he is enough. Islam and our Muslim friends put great faith in a dead prophet—and he is dead. You can visit his grave in Medina, Saudi Arabia. But Jesus Christ is alive! Our faith is in a risen Savior! May our Muslim friends come to know Jesus Christ and be transformed by him as well.

In the name of God the Father and God the Son and God the Holy Spirit. Amen.

CHAPTER 8
The Bible and Mohammad

A BIBLICAL LOOK AT ISLAM

SUNDAY, NOVEMBER 11, 2001

The series of messages I am preaching, entitled *A Biblical Look at Islam*, is not normal fare for an evangelical pulpit. So it is important, for those who regularly attend Calvary Baptist and those visiting, to know that I don't preach Mohammad—I never have and never will. I preach Christ. However, in order to share the truth of Christ, in love, with our Muslim co-workers, neighbors and friends, it helps to know what they believe. 9/11 is an unforgettable tragedy and an important teachable moment to demonstrate the difference between the God of the Bible and the God of Islam. They are not the same God. Jesus Christ is the Son of the living God—God in the flesh. He is greater than Moses; he is greater than Mohammad. Nevertheless, our Muslim friends continue to believe that Mohammad is the greatest of all prophets—greater than Jesus Christ.

In the Koran, Surah 33:40 says, "Mohammad is a messenger of God and the seal of the prophets." Islam teaches that there were many prophets before Mohammad. It recognizes and honors Jesus as a great prophet—yet insists that the last and greatest prophet of God was Mohammad and therefore refers to him as the "seal of the prophets," the greatest and final word from God. Mohammad literally claims that the Bible itself, both the Old and New Testament, prophesied that he would come as the apostle and prophet of God. In Surah 7:157 Allah is speaking and says:

> I will show mercy to those who shall follow the apostle, the unlettered (or Gentile) prophet, whom they shall find described to them in the Torah and the Gospel.

When Muslims claim that the Bible speaks of Mohammad, they are responsible to show where in the Bible Mohammad was prophesied. If they are going to make the claim then they have to back it up! Islam teaches that Mohammad was prophesied in two places in the Bible—one in both the Old and New Testaments. I want you to know these verses and understand that it is absolutely impossible that either verse refers to Mohammad! This is an important truth to share with your Muslim friends.

Islam claims that Mohammad is referred to in Deuteronomy, the fifth and last book of the Torah, the Law of Moses. Muslims believe Deuteronomy 18:15 predicted Mohammad's coming about 2000 years before he was born:

> The LORD your God will raise up for you a prophet like me from among you, from your brethren (fellow Israelites). You must listen to him.

Islam teaches that when Moses spoke this prophesy to the Jewish people he was saying that Mohammad would one day come and fulfill this prophecy. When you read on and consider the context, you realize this verse could not possibly be a prophecy about Mohammad:

> For this is what you asked of the LORD your God at Horeb on the day of the assembly when you said, "Let us not hear the voice of the LORD our God nor see this great fire any-more, or we will die." The LORD said to me: "What they say is good. I will raise up for them a prophet like you from among their brethren (fellow Israelites), and I will put my

words in his mouth. He will tell them everything I command him." (Deut. 18:16-18)

God says that this prophet who is coming will be a true prophet, like Moses. He will prove his authenticity by speaking God's Word. Notice what follows:

> I myself will call to account anyone who does not listen to my words that the prophet speaks in my name. But a prophet who presumes to speak in my name anything I have not commanded, or a prophet who speaks in the name of other gods, is to be put to death. You may say to yourselves, "How can we know when a message has not been spoken by the LORD?" If what a prophet proclaims in the name of the LORD does not take place or come true, that is a message the LORD has not spoken. That prophet has spoken presumptuously, so do not be alarmed. (Deut. 18:19-22)

God says a true prophet is coming, like Moses, and he will speak the Word of God—so you better listen to him! But beware of any one who comes along and claims to be that prophet while contradicting the truth of what God has said!

What is so interesting when you read the Koran is that it is filled with references from the Bible. Some of what is taught in the Koran about the Old and New Testament is actually accurate. For instance, Mohammad taught in the Koran that Jesus Christ was a prophet of God and that he was literally born of a virgin—and this is true. However, there is much more in the Koran that is false and contradicts the Bible.

The Bible teaches that Jesus Christ is God in the flesh. The Koran denies it and rejects the deity of Christ as blasphemy! The Bible teaches that Jesus Christ died on the cross for our sins, as the atonement. The Koran and Islam utterly reject this truth. The Bible teaches that Jesus Christ rose bodily from the dead. The Koran denies the resurrection of Jesus. The Koran does teach, however, that Jesus Christ will come again, which is true—but also teaches that Jesus Christ will come again to proclaim Islam, which is false. So Mohammad and the Koran are half right. Jesus will come again, but not to proclaim Islam! This is important because God says that whoever this prophet is who is like Moses, when he speaks, his message will be perfectly consistent with the message of the God who spoke to Moses. So Islam has a problem when it claims to be biblical! How can Mohammad be the prophet like Moses when much of what he says contradicts what the Bible says? Now the response of our Muslim friends is—God did give the Old and New Testament originally but they became corrupted and are no longer trustworthy; therefore, God had to give the Koran to make it all clear again. This is Islam's desperate attempt to deflect attention from the questions surrounding the transmission and corruption of the Koran over the centuries. As for the Bible, textual criticism has demonstrated the accurate and trustworthy translation and transmission of the scriptures.

Could Mohammad possibly have been this prophet like Moses? No way! His message totally contradicts Moses and Jesus Christ! There's even more trouble for Islam in this context:

> The LORD your God will raise up for you a prophet like me
> from your midst, from *your brethren* (fellow Israelites). Him
> you shall hear. (Deuteronomy 18:15, NKJ)

Whoever this prophet is will be from Moses' brethren—his fellow Israelites. Now we realize that Moses was a Hebrew. He was a part of the nation of Israel. In response to this, Islam correctly asserts that Abraham, an ancestor of Moses, was not only the father of the Jewish people, but also the father of the Arabs through Ishmael—and that's all true! So which *brethren* will this prophet, who is like Moses, actually come from and identify with? A larger context will help us answer the question.

Deuteronomy 13 addresses the issue of true and false prophets:

> If a prophet, or one who foretells by dreams, appears among
> you and announces to you a sign or wonder, and if the sign or
> wonder spoken of takes place, and the prophet says, "*Let us
> follow other gods (gods you have not known) and let us wor-
> ship them*," you must not listen to the words of that prophet

or dreamer. The LORD your God is testing you to find out
whether you love him with all your heart and with all your soul.
(Deuteronomy 13:1-4 NIV)

In this context, the Hebrew people are ready to enter the Promised
Land, and God through Moses has given them last minute instructions
about how they are going to live in this new world. He warns them to
watch out for all the idols in the Promised Land. The Canaanites are worshipping all kinds of gods—just like in New York City today. God says
that if a prophet says he is prophesying in my name, the true God, but he
then encourages you to follow another god or idol, you know for sure he
is not speaking from me.

It is true, both biblically and historically, that Allah is not the God of
the Bible. Therefore, you can make a strong case that Mohammad is calling everyone to follow a god that the nation Israel in the Old Testament
did not know and the church of the New Testament does not know. It's
important to understand this.

The context is that Israel is going into the land and God is warning his
people, the new nation of Israel—don't get caught up in idolatry. Deuteronomy 14:1 says, "You are the children of the LORD your God." Who
is God referring to here? Clearly, he is referring to the nation Israel; the
people of the covenant that was given by God through Abraham, Isaac
and Jacob. God loved Hagar and Ishmael, and he loves the Arab people,
but the covenant of God was made with Israel and the Jewish people,
through whom the Messiah, Jesus Christ, would come.

You are the children of the LORD your God. Do not cut yourselves or shave the front of your heads for the dead... (Deuteronomy 14:1)

He said don't engage in idolatrous practices like the Canaanite tribes
because:

You are a people holy to the LORD your God. Out of all the
peoples on the face of the earth, the LORD has chosen you to be
his treasured possession. (Deuteronomy 14:2)

A Time *for* Hope

This chosen people, this treasured possession is Israel. In Deuteronomy 15:12 the context gets more specific:

> If any of your people—Hebrew men or women—sell themselves to you and serve you six years, in the seventh year you must let them go free.

The LORD is speaking of the Hebrew people when he says, "I will raise up a prophet like you from among your brethren" (Deut. 18:15). The seventh year was the year that the slaves would be freed—the Year of Jubilee. I am spending some time on this because it is important to see clearly who the brethren are and what the context is:

> Observe the month of Aviv and celebrate the Passover of the LORD your God, because in the month of Aviv he brought you out of Egypt by night. Sacrifice as the Passover to the LORD your God an animal from your flock or herd at the place the LORD will choose as a dwelling for his Name. (Deut 16:1-2)

Now, who is he speaking to? It's the Hebrew nation that was in bondage in Egypt. God in the Passover took the life of the first born in each Egyptian family and protected the Hebrews because of the blood of the sacrificed lamb applied to their doorposts, which pointed to the Messiah who would come from the Jewish people. God led them out in the Exodus and set them free. Clearly the *brethren* are the Jewish people and nation:

> When you come to the land which the LORD your God is giving you, and possess it and dwell in it, and say, "I will set a king over me like all the nations that *are* around me," you shall surely set a king over you whom the LORD your God chooses; *one* from among **your brethren** you shall set as king over you; you may not set a foreigner over you, who is not your brother. (Deut. 17:14-15, NKJ)

There again, the *brethren* refer to the Hebrews, the tribes of Israel:

> The priests, the Levites—all the tribe of Levi—shall have no part, nor inheritance with Israel; they shall eat the offerings of

the LORD made by fire, and his portion. Therefore they shall have no inheritance among *their brethren*; the LORD is their inheritance, as he said to them. (Deuteronomy 18:1-2, NKJ)

This is unequivocally referring to the Jewish people and the nation Israel:

The LORD your God will raise up for you a prophet like me from your midst, from your brethren. Him you shall hear. (Deuteronomy 18:15)

Clearly the prophet that Moses prophesied would come would be Jewish. And clearly that prophecy was pointing not to Mohammad — but to the Messiah, Jesus Christ. That was the understanding of the early church also.

In Acts 7 we read about Stephen, the very first martyr of the Christian church described in the New Testament. In the face of Jewish disbelief and opposition, Stephen is reviewing, for the opponents of the gospel, the glorious and tragic history of Israel. He shows that the Old Testament scriptures were constantly saying that the Messiah was coming. Therefore, Stephen says in Acts 7:37:

This is that Moses who said to the children of Israel, "The LORD your God will raise up for you a prophet like me from *your brethren*. Him you shall hear."

This is Stephen interpreting Deuteronomy 18:15, under the guidance of the Holy Spirit. The one promised all along by Moses was not going to be Mohammad 600 years later, but Jesus of Nazareth. Stephen continues:

...you stiff-necked and uncircumcised in heart and ears! You always resist the Holy Spirit; as your fathers did, so do you. Which of the prophets did your fathers not persecute? (Acts 7:51-52)

The Jewish people have been the most blessed and the most cursed people in the history of the world. Most blessed because they are God's people; most cursed because they rejected their own Messiah and God's wrath and judgment came upon them—but one day "all Israel will be saved." (Romans 11:26)

The gospel is the love of God for the Jews, Muslims, Christians, Hindus, Buddhists, agnostics, atheists and everyone else! The Messiah Jesus was a Jew, born to a people blessed and cursed by God! So who was this prophet that Moses prophesied? He is Jesus Christ.

Stephen continues:

> And they killed those who foretold the coming of the Just One, of whom you now have become the betrayers and murderers, who have received the law by the direction of angels and have not kept it.

> When they heard these things they were cut to the heart, and they gnashed at him with their teeth. But he, being full of the Holy Spirit, gazed into heaven and saw the glory of God, and Jesus standing at the right hand of God, and said, "Look! I see the heavens opened and the Son of Man standing at the right hand of God!" (Acts 7:53-56)

Jesus is the prophet like Moses that God promised:

> At this they covered their ears and yelling at the top of their voices they all rushed at him, dragged him out of the city and began to stone him. Meanwhile, the witnesses laid their coats at the feet of a young man named Saul. (Acts 7:57-58)

Saul was a Jewish Pharisee, a religious terrorist, a man who spent years persecuting and killing many who believed in Jesus Christ. Then the terrorist encountered Jesus Christ on the road to Damascus, Syria, and was transformed into an apostle of love! This is what we focused on the very first Sunday after 9/11—the hope that God can also bring the terrorists in our day to the foot of the cross, in utter repentance and sorrow for their sin, and turn their hearts around. He saved us, didn't He? We have all been terrorists in our own way. We all have a few people in our life who could say, "Oh yeah, you hurt me. You killed me softly—but you killed me anyway." There are terrorists in our homes, our workplace, and even our churches! We've all done it—been there, done that! The only way for a terrorist, foreign or domestic, to become compassionate is to meet the living God in Jesus Christ. Jesus is the prophet of Deuteronomy 18:15, greater than Moses and greater than Mohammad! You must share this truth lovingly with your Jewish and Muslim friends and neighbors. The prophet has come—and his name is Jesus!

Mohammad also claimed that Jesus *himself* prophesied that he (Mohammad) would come. In the Koran, Surah 61:6 Mohammad says:

> Jesus says to the Israelites, "I am sent from God to confirm the Torah and to give news of an apostle who will come after me whose name is Ahmed or Mohammad."

The Koran says Jesus came to confirm Deuteronomy 18:15 in the Torah, and to also announce the coming of Mohammad in John 14:16-18:

> And I will ask the Father, and he will give you another advocate (comforter) to help you and be with you forever— the Spirit of truth. The world cannot accept him, because it neither sees him nor knows him. But you know him, for he lives with you and will be in you. I will not leave you as orphans; I will come to you. (John 14:16-18, NIV)

These are amazing verses and when understood correctly, the way Jesus intended them, they communicate a profound truth—but this truth is not about Mohammad.

In his book, The Islam Debate, Josh McDowell offers a number of reasons why these verses cannot possibly refer to Mohammad. I have summarized them for you:

1. "And I will ask the Father, and he will give *you* another Comforter..." The promise was to the apostles on the night before Jesus was crucified. Mohammad, who

came 600 years later, could not be the fulfillment of a promise made to the apostles.

2. "And I will ask the Father, and he will give you another *Comforter*…" Jesus promised an encourager, an advocate, a paraclete—not the "promised one" as Muslims like to refer to Mohammad.

3. "And I will ask the Father, and he will give you another advocate (comforter) to help you and *be with you forever*…" Mohammad lived 62 years, which was a long time back then. But 62 years is a long way from forever!

4. "And I will ask the Father, and he will give you another advocate (comforter) to help you and be with you forever— *the Spirit of truth.*" Jesus promised a spirit being, the Holy Spirit—not a human being, Mohammad.

5. "The *world cannot accept him*…" Sadly, the entire human race will not receive the Holy Spirit because it will not receive Jesus—but Islam will attempt to force everyone to accept Mohammad.

6. "…because it neither sees him nor knows him. *But you know him.*" The apostles knew this Comforter, the Holy Spirit. They couldn't know Mohammad who was born 600 years later.

7. "…for he lives with you and *will be in you.*" Only a spirit being can live inside a person. Mohammad doesn't qualify.

These New Testament verses, which are used by Islam to attempt to prove that Jesus promised the coming of Mohammad cannot possibly, by any stretch of the imagination, refer to Mohammad! I encourage you to read Josh McDowell's book carefully. It will strengthen your witness to Muslims.

Islam also asserts that in John 15:26 Jesus himself speaks about Mohammad:

> But when the Comforter is come, whom I will send unto you from the Father, even the Spirit of truth, which proceeds from the Father, he shall testify of me. (NKJ)

First of all, it is inconsistent for Islam to claim that the Comforter is Mohammad, when Islam totally repudiates the idea that God is a Father. How can God the Father, who is rejected by Islam, be the one who sends Mohammad? For Muslims it is blasphemy to refer to God as a Father who has a Son. So for Islam to claim that God the Father sent his Son to announce Mohammad contradicts every belief of Islam. It is contradictory, illogical and irrational for Islam to make this claim.

The Holy Spirit is the Comforter that Jesus promises—not Mohammad. The Holy Spirit is the "Spirit of truth." This means that everything the Comforter says is going to be true. Jesus says, "He will testify about me." So our Muslim friends are saying that Jesus promised the Comforter who would be Mohammad, but the text says the purpose of the Comforter is to *only* talk about Jesus Christ. Obviously, Mohammad didn't do this. He didn't talk much about Jesus Christ—he talked a lot more about himself! So he couldn't possibly fulfill this promise.

Jesus continues in his upper room discourse:

> Nevertheless I tell you the truth. It is to your advantage that I go away; for if I do not go away, the Helper will not come to you; but if I depart, I will send him to you. And when he has come, he will convict the world of sin, and of righteousness, and of judgment: of sin, because they do not believe in me; of righteousness, because I go to my Father and you see me no more; of judgment, because the ruler of this world is judged. (John 16:7-11, NKJ)

The Holy Spirit is going to convict the human race because they don't believe in Jesus—not because they reject Mohammad! Islam teaches just

the opposite: the world is guilty and under judgment because they don't
believe in Allah or his prophet.

Jesus says the Spirit always tells the truth!

> However, when He, the Spirit of truth, has come, he will guide
> you into ***all truth***. (John 16:13, NKJ)

Most of what Mohammad says contradicts what Moses and Jesus say.
That's a long way from *all truth*!

Jesus continues teaching about the Holy Spirit:

> He will not speak on his own *authority,* but whatever he hears
> he will speak; and he will tell you things to come. He will glo-
> rify me, for he will take of what is mine and declare *it* to you.
> (John 16:13-14, NKJ)

Jesus says that the Holy Spirit is going to take what is his and make
it known to us. Mohammad took what belongs to Jesus, but instead of
making it known to us, he twisted and corrupted it. It is interesting that
although Mohammad claims that the Bible had become corrupted and
Allah sent him to set the record straight—it is actually Mohammad himself who corrupts and twists the scriptures. Therefore, Jesus is greater
than Mohammad; and the Bible, the written Word of God, is superior
to the Koran.

If you are here today without Jesus but are considering his claims, realize that the God and Father of the Lord Jesus Christ is a great God. He
is transcendent. He is high and lifted up. He is greater than we are—his
thoughts are greater than our thoughts. He is also the God who loves
us personally. He is Immanuel—God with us. This God who is awesome and mighty is also personal, approachable, and can be known. He
is unlike the God of Islam who remains distant, impersonal and unknowable. They are not the same God. I say this lovingly and respectfully but
categorically and unapologetically. The God of Islam cannot save anyone.

In contrast, the God of the Bible, who created the universe and reveals himself in his only Son Jesus Christ, not only can save—but does save, if we will pray and ask for his mercy and grace:

> Dear Lord God, thank you for loving me in spite of my sin. Thank you that when my sin abounded, your grace abounded more. Thank you that when I was in rebellion against you, you didn't ask me to clean up my act first and then you would love me; but literally in the midst of my rebellion, when I was in your face—you loved me, and Christ died for me in the midst of my rebellion. I repent of my sins. I believe Jesus died for my sins and rose from the dead to forgive me. Lord Jesus I receive you now—have mercy on me a sinner.

It is only the truth that sets people free. Jesus said:

> You shall know the truth and the truth shall make you free... whoever commits sin is a slave of sin. And a slave does not abide in the house forever, but a son abides forever. Therefore, if the Son makes you free, you shall be free indeed. (John 8:32, 34-36)

No wonder Jesus can say emphatically:

> I am the Way, the Truth and the Life, no man comes to the Father except through me. (John 14:6)

The only way to God, according to Jesus, is through him—through his love, his cross and his empty tomb! Do not turn your back on the grace of God today!

May the Lord revive his people again—those of us who have tasted his grace. May God also use us to revive our city and nation. May we experience love, joy and power because Jesus Christ lives and intercedes for us. Jesus is not ashamed to call us "his brethren." In Christ we can now cry out "Abba Father" to God. May our Muslim neighbors come to know

Jesus as their Lord and Savior. Remember that one day "every knee shall bow, and every tongue will confess that Jesus Christ is Lord to the glory of God the Father." (Philippians 2:10-11) I encourage you to bow your knee now and confess Jesus as Lord—while there is still time.

In the name of God the Father and God the Son and God the Holy Spirit. Amen.

CHAPTER 9
The Path to Paradise

A BIBLICAL LOOK AT ISLAM

SUNDAY, NOVEMBER 18, 2001

This Thanksgiving I'm grateful that God loves me and that by his grace I know his Son Jesus Christ. God loved me when I was confused, discouraged, disillusioned and alienated from everyone and everything. I was unsure of who I was, where I came from, why I was here, and what life was all about. I am really glad that God in his grace loved me when I was unlovable and reached out to me long before I ever desired to reach out to him. As a matter of fact, God reached out to me when I had my fist in his face! I'm grateful that I worship a God who is transcendent, awesome and mighty. He is greater than I am. He is God and I am not. That's the one thing I know for sure. He is Immanuel—God with us. I am grateful that I can worship the God who said:

> In the beginning was the Word, and the Word was with God and the Word was God…and the Word became flesh and dwelt among us. (John 1:1, 14)

Jesus Christ came in solidarity with us, identified with us, and took the hit for us. I rejoice in the fact that Calvary Baptist Church can love, pray for and share Christ with our Muslim friends, relatives, co-workers and cab drivers! I have had the privilege of speaking about Jesus Christ with Muslim cab drivers from Bangladesh, Pakistan, Egypt, Sierra Leone, Sudan, India, Nigeria—just to name a few! They acknowledge that their God Allah is a distant and impersonal God who cannot be known. What can be known about Allah is his will, revealed by Mohammad and the Koran. A Muslim must be in submission to the will of Allah.

I thank God that we have the privilege of being witnesses of Christ to the Muslim community in New York City. We can speak the truth in love and share with them that God's name is *I AM WHO I AM*. He created us all and offers everyone forgiveness and redemption in Jesus Christ. I thank God that I can follow a prophet and an apostle, Jesus Christ, who has proven himself through the centuries to be the greatest spiritual leader, teacher, and moral example who ever lived. Jesus is affirmed by the Bible, by history and even by the Koran as spiritually and morally superior to Mohammad –because even Islam teaches that Jesus was without sin, but Mohammad was a sinful man. History documents that Mohammad killed people in war; he kidnapped men, women and children and held them for ransom. He was guilty of revenge killing, forced conversions, and slave trading. I want to be able to tell Muslims, not in condemnation but in love, "How about Jesus?" How can you say that Mohammad came as the final and greatest prophet when you actually compare Jesus and Mohammad? Look at the contrast in the way they lived, what they taught, and the example they set! Clearly Jesus is the greater prophet.

Jesus was the one spoken of in John 1:14, "We have beheld his glory, the glory as of the only begotten of the Father, full of grace and truth." When you search and study history and world religions, you learn that the only place you find God's liberating and transforming grace is in Jesus the Messiah. We want to share him with Muslims everywhere.

I am thankful that I follow the holy book, the Bible, which is actually inspired by God, infallible and life changing. Islam believes that the Bible was originally given by God but was later corrupted and the Koran took its place. Islam also claims that the Bible prophesied Mohammad's coming in both the Old and New Testament. When we evaluate these verses we discover that there is no way in the world — exegetically, historically or logically — that the Bible ever mentions Mohammad! The Bible, however, does speak of the Messiah, Jesus Christ, from Genesis 1 to Revelation 22.

When you contrast the history, origin and transmission of the Bible with the Koran, you see an enormous quantitative and qualitative difference. The Bible was communicated by God over a period of 1600 years — from 1500 BC to AD 100. God used more than 40 human authors who maintained a striking unity of purpose, a progression of thought, and an unfolding of God's redemptive plan. The Bible includes cosmology, poetry and prose, wisdom literature, drama, prophecy, history, apocalyptic, parable and story — all held together in a unified way covering 1600 years. That's a powerful book! The Koran was the product of one man, who was allegedly spoken to by God through an angel over a short period of 20 years. When you evaluate the Bible and the Koran honestly and objectively, the quantitative and qualitative superiority of the Bible is obvious.

Islam teaches that the Bible was corrupted in its transmission. This teaching is false. When you study the history of the transcription and transmission of the Old Testament by the Massoretes, the scribes, you find they showed tremendous care and diligence in handling the Scriptures. Then you see why Islam is wrong on this issue.

In fact, just this week the first entire edition of the Dead Sea Scrolls have been published. I had the privilege in some of my doctoral work to study at Catholic University under Dr. Joseph Fitzmyer, one of the leading experts in the Dead Sea Scrolls in the world. What an amazing accomplishment to get all of that published! What's interesting is that the Dead Sea Scrolls, which were written between 250 BC and AD 75, a period of over 300 years, contained much of the Old Testament as it was transmitted through the centuries.

A few years ago I was in Israel doing some teaching and leading a tour. While at Qumran, looking out at the caves where the Dead Sea Scrolls had been discovered, our Israeli guide was telling us how he had memorized a portion of Isaiah for his bar mitzvah as a Jewish teenager. He said, "I wonder how much the passage I read for my bar mitzvah has changed in 2000 years." So he went and compared the passage in Isaiah from the Dead Sea Scrolls with the passage he had memorized as a teenager and to his amazement they were identical—2300 years later! Word for word, consonant for consonant! The Lord Jesus said, "Heaven and earth will pass away but my words will never pass away." (Matthew 24:35)

I want our Muslim friends to know that every verse of the Bible is inspired by God. (2 Timothy 3:16) This is vitally important as we share the gospel with Muslims, who worship another God called Allah. Allah used to be the moon-god, an idol in pre-Islamic Mecca. Muslims also follow a different prophet, Mohammad, and obey a different holy book, the Koran. Therefore Muslims come to another idea of salvation—in fact, a very different idea about salvation. The Islamic concept of salvation, in a general sense, is not unique. The religions of the world have always taught a *works* salvation—what can I do to work my way back to God, whoever and wherever he is? Islam, however, presents a variation on the theme of finding our way back to God by man's own efforts. Islam teaches that we must earn Allah's favor and forgiveness, hoping against hope that we will be accepted in the end. In the history of world religion, earning our forgiveness by our own works is the norm; grace is the exception. Grace is the anomaly! The only place you find the unmerited grace of God is in Jesus Christ. The only time in history you find God himself working his way to us, when we could never work our way to him, is in the cross of Jesus Christ. Jesus Christ is the greatest gift God ever gave to the human race. True salvation is always undeserved and unearned! That's what makes grace so *amazing*! What an awesome gospel we have the privilege of sharing in this day and age.

We need to understand how Muslims define salvation so we can more effectively communicate the gospel to them. Muslims are taught to perform the Five Pillars of Islam. There are actually Six Pillars when you include jihad.

The first pillar of Islam is the creed or confession. Every Muslim must confess that Allah is the one true God and that Mohammad is his messenger, his prophet. This is the first thing a Muslim must do to be accepted by Allah.

The second pillar of Islam is the required prayers. Muslims are required to pray five times a day in a prescribed way—facing Mecca.

The third pillar of Islam is the giving of alms. Muslims are required to give 2.5% of their income to the poor.

The fourth pillar is fasting. Muslims have a special month of fasting called Ramadan which culminates in the Feast of Ramadan. They fast the entire month, not eating food from sunrise to sunset.

The fifth Pillar of Islam is the Hajj or Pilgrimage. Every Muslim, at one time in his life, if able, must make a holy visit to Mecca in Saudi Arabia, to the Kaaba, which is the number one place of worship in Islam. The Hajj can be a difficult challenge if you are a poor Muslim and live a long distance away on another continent and want to visit Mecca before you die. You can imagine the pressure and fear people must feel if they believe Paradise is at stake.

A few months ago I was in a cab and I had a driver who was a young man from Pakistan. As I often do, I started a conversation with him. We were talking about our kids, which is a nice way to break the ice. Then we talked about how we all want our children to get a good education. I said to him, "Do you teach your kids at home about your prophet Mohammad?" He said, "Yes, it's important to teach them spiritually and religiously." Then I said, "You know, I have been reading your Koran about your prophet. Have you ever read the Bible about my prophet?" He said, "No, I've never really looked at a Bible." I said, "Have you obeyed all the Pillars of Islam? Have you made a pilgrimage to Mecca yet?" He said, "No, but I have to do it. I'm trying to save money, but it's very expensive." And then he got personal and said, "You know some of the rich people over in the Middle East, they don't have any problem. They have money and they are not far away. They can make the Hajj every year if they want. But for a guy like me, I am a taxi driver and I have a family—

it's hard to get money. It's very hard and yet I need to get there." And then I said, "You know it's an amazing thing, my Prophet, Jesus, offers us a relationship with God through his cross. God offers us forgiveness for our sins by his grace if we will believe in Jesus —and this salvation is free. You don't need to spend any money." He said, "That's interesting." I repeated to him, "It's free! Salvation is free. It's all about grace." That really surprised him.

God loves us. He is gracious. He offers us a relationship with himself—the Living God. He doesn't keep us in terror all our lives, wondering if we can be good enough, and serve him enough, and raise enough money to get to some holy site so he might accept us. In Islam there is no assurance of forgiveness and salvation because Allah does not have to be true to his own character. He can do whatever he wants. He doesn't even have to honor his own word. In Islam, Allah is often believed to be the author of evil itself as well as good. So how can you know Allah is going to be good to you? You can't! This lack of the assurance of salvation and entering Paradise in Islam is a real problem. That's why a sixth pillar of Islam is added—jihad.

Jihad is an interesting concept. It is about warfare but not just physical warfare. Jihad also means the struggle to live life in submission to Allah. In the Christian life also we are challenged to "work out our salvation with fear and trembling. For it is God who works in you both to will and to do for his good pleasure." (Philippians 2:12-13) Jesus Christ calls the Christian to sanctification, discipleship and spiritual warfare. However, there is an element of jihad which is very Muslim and characterizes Islam. It is why Islam is known as the religion of the sword.

We talked earlier about the first hundred years of Islamic history, which saw its rapid expansion through war and terror—jihad! Jihad is when a Muslim is called to faithfully wage war to defend Islam against infidels and to propagate the faith by force. This means that in situations where Islam feels threatened by another nation, people or culture, they will call a jihad. Jihad is the only pillar of Islam where Mohammad promises to those who obey it an absolute certainty of entering Paradise—the only one! Islam promises Paradise to these young men who are blowing themselves up to serve Allah! Islam promises them a carnal Paradise, a real man's Paradise—not some spiritual "nonsense." Islam promises these young men, who are mostly 18-30 years old, that when they kill and die in the name of Allah, they will enjoy beautiful virgins forever. You may ask, "Pastor Dave, this sounds naïve. I mean does anyone really believe this stuff?" It makes sense if you are raised as a kid in this Islamic system all your life and you live in fear of death if you blaspheme Mohammad or Allah! Then you are told as a young man, just as you begin to physically mature and experience sexual feelings and desires—if you strap on that bomb and work for Allah and are killed in jihad, you will go to Paradise and boy will you be happy in Paradise! The abuse and manipulation of these young men is horrific and dishonors God big time! And they strap those bombs on.

Now I am not saying that every young Muslim man is a terrorist. I have said repeatedly in other messages, that most Muslims are peace-loving people. But many Muslims are ignorant of the true nature of their own religion. They are ignorant of their own holy book and history. Islam is not a religion of peace. Historically it is the religion of jihad. That is why some young men are flying planes into the World Trade Center. They can't wait to get to Paradise and start a new life! They want to serve Allah and build an Islamic world, and dying in jihad furthers the cause. The Koran encourages them to kill and die for Allah—promising them Paradise if they do.

Bin Laden in one of his recent video tapes said, "If avenging the killing of our people is terrorism then history should be a witness that we are terrorists." And history has been a witness that Islam engages in terror. There have been times throughout history when Christians have also pursued terror. What makes all the difference, however, is that when Christians have engaged in terror, it is always diametrically opposed to the teaching and the personal example of Jesus Christ. Tragically, when Muslims engage in terror it is consistent with Mohammad's own teaching and personal example. The contrast could not be more graphic!

A TIME *for* HOPE

Bin Laden has called on Muslims to join his jihad or holy war saying: "It is the duty of every Muslim to fight, and killing Jews is our top priority." He also included Americans in many other statements he made as well. This is jihad. This is historic Islam.

God loves the Muslim and Arab people just like he loves us. God saved us when we were morally rebellious and in his face. He saved Paul when he was terrorizing Christians in the first century. Paul was a terrorist and a murderer. He actually believed he was serving God! Then God in his sovereign grace and purpose brought him to repentance and faith in Christ, and he was transformed. This is what God desires to do for Islamic terrorists who pursue jihad against Americans and Jews and children as well. God wants to bring them to repentance for their sins and to faith in Jesus Christ. Thank God for the gospel of Jesus Christ that transforms the hearts and minds of terrorists.

Muslims believe they must work hard to gain Allah's favor by obeying the six pillars of Islam. In contrast, Christians believe that salvation is the gift of God by faith in Jesus Christ. The difference is 180 degrees! Nevertheless, Islam does actually teach some important truths about Jesus, which can serve as bridges in sharing Jesus with Muslims.

For instance, Islam teaches that Jesus Christ is a Messiah. He is an anointed one of God. Muslims believe this. They believe that Jesus lived a sinless life. They believe that Jesus was born of a virgin. Now they don't understand this biblically, because Islam claims it is blasphemy to think of God as a Father having a Son; therefore Muslims don't see God conceiving a child with Mary, in the sense of the Holy Spirit begetting Jesus within her womb. They simply see it as an act of Allah from a distance where an impersonal God basically says, "Mary's going to have a child and she is going to be a virgin—make it be." Just like that—hands off, at a distance. The important thing is that Muslims believe in the virgin birth. So this is a place where you can talk about how God came to identify with the human race.

Islam teaches that Jesus Christ is alive today with God. Muslims believe that Jesus Christ is coming back a second time. Of course, they believe that he is coming back to proclaim Islam, which he is not! He is coming back to be the King of Kings and the Lord of Lords. At that time every knee shall bow — Moses, Zoroaster, Confucius, Mohammad, the Dalai Lama — and every tongue shall confess that Jesus Christ is Lord to the glory of God the Father. (Philippians 2:10) Islam teaches that Jesus is coming back again.

What is tragic is that while Muslims believe many truths about Jesus Christ, they reject the most important things. They reject the truth that Jesus Christ is the Son of God. They say its blasphemy, it's a perversion that God could have a Son. They reject the fatherhood of God. They say that God can't be a father; rather, Allah is a distant force, a mysterious personality, unknowable and unapproachable. Muslims do not believe that Jesus went to the cross and died as a substitute for our sins. They reject the cross and the atonement and the fact that Jesus was crucified as a sin-offering. Islam rejects the truth that Jesus was raised bodily from the dead in a powerful, physical, historical resurrection. Islam denies the deity of Jesus, his atonement and his resurrection. Islam rejects the gospel — therefore, most Muslims reject it also.

It's interesting that in Mecca, when the pilgrims come to worship Allah during the Hajj, they have a ceremony where they actually dramatize the offering of Ishmael by Abraham. They believe the Koran teaches them, in contradiction to the Bible, that Abraham offered Ishmael instead of Isaac. In this drama, they actually offer an animal sacrifice. What they don't understand is that when this event took place about 2000 BC with Abraham and Isaac, as Abraham began to bring the knife down to slay his son, God stopped him. God was saying, "No, I'm testing your faith! It's not your son I want. I want your obedience, which is prophetic, and points people 2000 years into the future when I will offer my son, Jesus Christ, on Calvary's cross as an atonement for sins." That's why Abraham said to Isaac, "God himself will provide the lamb for the sacrifice." (Genesis 22:8) What our Jewish and Muslim friends need to understand is that when Abraham offered Isaac, God was saying one day he was going to offer his only Son, and in that day when the knife comes down there will be no hand to stay it! This time God will offer his own Son for the Jew, the Muslim and the Christian. This is an awesome, powerful truth. By God's grace may our Jewish and Muslim neighbors come to that knowledge and understanding and bow before that cross.

The Bible is the written revelation of God. The theme of Scripture from Genesis to Revelation is the love and grace of God offered to the human race through the Messiah, Jesus Christ. Luke 24 gives us a summary of this wonderful redemptive history. The time is Easter Sunday, the day of Jesus' resurrection, and two people, Cleopas and an unnamed companion, are returning from Jerusalem to Emmaus. They had been *hoping* that Jesus would be raised from the dead and God would usher in his kingdom, but they hadn't yet seen the risen Christ and they were discouraged. Jesus appeared to them on the Emmaus road but they were kept from recognizing Him. In Luke 24:25 Jesus says:

> "O foolish ones, and slow of heart to believe in all that the prophets have spoken! Ought not the Christ to have suffered these things and to enter into his glory?" And beginning at Moses and all the prophets, he expounded to them in all the Scriptures the things concerning *himself.* (Luke 24:25-27)

This is the teaching of Jesus, the one Islam claims to honor. Jesus Christ is the focus of the entire Bible! Jesus tells us himself that the Bible is all about him. No wonder the Bible demonstrates such a profound unity of theme and purpose. No wonder the Bible so accurately describes the progressive unfolding of God's redemptive plan in history. God created history and he chose the Jewish people and the nation of Israel to bear his name and show his glory. Tragically, they rejected their own Messiah; therefore, God raised up the church, which includes both Jews and Gentiles, to show his glory and bear witness to his name. One day he will consummate history in the second coming of Jesus and establish his earthly and eternal kingdoms. What a day that's going to be! What a profound biblical world view and philosophy of history! It's astounding! The Bible is about Jesus Christ. No wonder the Scriptures held together over 1600 years with 40 plus authors—because the Messiah, Jesus Christ, is the theme of the Bible.

It's vital that we contrast the Pillars of Islam with the Biblical salvation offered by a loving, gracious God. In John 6:28 some in the crowd asked Jesus, "What must we do to do the works God requires?" What a great question!

Now if these same people had lived 600 years later instead of when Jesus was alive, they might have asked that same question to Mohammad. They might have said, "Prophet, what must we do to do the works of God?" And Mohammad would have said, "Listen to me well—you need to confess that there's no God but Allah, and Mohammad is his prophet. Then you need to pray five times a day and give alms, 2.5% of your income. Then you need to fast and honor Ramadan and make a holy pilgrimage to Mecca." And they would say, "Prophet, if we do all these things will we be assured of Paradise?" And he would have to say, "No, because who knows what Allah will do. But this is what Allah wants. But if you die in battle with Allah's enemies you will be assured of Paradise." This would have been his answer to that question. Now let's go back to Jesus:

> Jesus answered, "The work of God is this: *to believe in the one he has sent*." (John 6:29)

What an awesome response! This is the work of God—honor the Son, believe in him, take hold of him by faith, cling to his cross. Trust that he has satisfied God's holiness and set the captives free. What a gospel! The gospel of salvation by grace through faith—just believe in him.

We have been getting hundreds of letter since September 11th. We have been getting thousands of letters since three years ago when we increased our radio ministry to six days a week. It never ceases to thrill and amaze me how God continues to say, "Believe in the one whom I have sent." We got a letter this week that said:

> Dear Calvary, I am just blessed by how God is using you. Just by listening to your program and what God had to say through

you, my life has completely turned around. I am in prison for the last 3 years. I want to express my love and gratitude for the support you give to prisoners listening to your program. Because of your ministry I am able to maintain my Christian walk while incarcerated. It really helps when things look hopeless. By the grace of God, he has chosen me here in my unit to preach his word and placed me as the pastor of 15-20 men. We meet every night in the name of Jesus.

Mohammad says practice the six pillars and Jesus says, "Believe in the one who he sent." The grace of God. Here is a letter from Campus Crusade and their Muslim ministry:

Let's begin with an amazing report from a Muslim country where we have been advertising the Jesus Film. A man called and asked for a video from a Muslim country, but he said, "Not through the mail. Please bring it in person at 2 p.m." A volunteer found the address and knocked on the door. A man in flowing robes answered, a Muslim cleric. The volunteer apologized profusely, "I am sorry to disturb you. I must have the wrong address." He was ready to leave when the Muslim Mullah asked, "Why are you here." He said, "Someone ordered a video cassette but I must have the wrong address." He said, "What cassette is it." Hesitantly the Christian worker said, "It's the story of Jesus, the Jesus Film." He said, "Well, you have the right house. I'm the one who ordered it." As he received the tape and turned to walk back inside the volunteer peered through the door. The room was filled with Muslim Mullahs, holy men, clerics. To a packed house of waiting people, this cleric explained, "Jesus has arrived, Jesus has arrived, we've got him!"

In John 8, six hundred years before Mohammad, another group of people had rejected Jesus Christ—our Jewish friends. And in John 8:52 some of the Jewish leaders said this to Jesus:

At this they exclaimed, "Now we know that you are demon-possessed! Abraham died and so did the prophets, yet you say that whoever obeys your word will never taste death. Are you greater than our father Abraham? He died, and so did the prophets. Who do you think you are?" (John 8:52-53)

Another very good question by the way!

Jesus replied, "If I glorify myself, my glory means nothing. My Father, whom you claim as your God, is the one who glorifies me. Though you do not know him, I know him. If I said I did not, I would be a liar like you, but I do know him and obey his word. Your father Abraham rejoiced at the thought of seeing my day; he saw it and was glad."

"You are not yet fifty years old," they said to him, "and you have seen Abraham?" "I tell you the truth," Jesus answered, "*before Abraham was born, I am!*" (John 8:54-58, NIV)

This is why he says today, "*I AM* the light of the world." This is why he says in John 10, "*I AM* the door...I AM the gate of the sheep." This is why he says, "*I AM* the Good Shepherd. The Good Shepherd gives his life for the sheep." This is why in John 11 when Martha and Mary were agonizing over the death of their brother Lazarus and said, "Lord, our brother wouldn't have died if you had been here." Jesus replied, "He will rise again." And Martha said, "I know that he will rise again in resurrection at the last day." Jesus said, "*I AM* the resurrection and the life—he who believes in me, though he die, yet shall he live. And he who lives and believes in me will never die. Do you believe this?" And Martha replied, "Yes Lord, I believe that you are the Christ the Son of God who is to come into the world." (John 11:20-27)

In John 14 after Thomas says, "Lord, we don't know where you are going, so how can we know the way?" (John 14:5) Jesus says:

A TIME *for* HOPE

I AM the way and the truth and the life. No one comes to the
Father except through me. (John 14:6)

That's an act of love, telling us the truth. If you are still without Christ
today, this is a gracious moment for you. God has given you a divine
appointment today. He has given you another chance to know that there
is no hope anywhere except in Jesus of Nazareth, Son of God, Messiah,
King of Kings and Lord of Lords, High Priest and Apostle. He is the
Logos, the Word who became flesh and "We beheld his glory, the glory of
the only son of the Father full of grace and truth." (John 1:14) Don't turn
your back and walk away from the grace of God today. Jesus is saying,
"Come to Me." The only prayer you need is, "Lord Jesus, remember me.
Have mercy on me a sinner. Forgive me. Make me new. Set me free.
Give me *hope*." And you will have a new life!

As for those of us who are followers of Christ today, our prayer should
be, "Lord Jesus, revive my witness. Make it bold. Make it loving. Make
it informed, knowledgeable and passionate." And remember—he always
answers these prayers with "Yes" and "Amen."

In the name of God the Father and God the Son and God the Holy
Spirit. Amen.

ACKNOWLEDGMENTS

I want to acknowledge those who have encouraged me in writing this book:

First and foremost I thank my beautiful wife, Sandy, who stole my heart the first moment I met her. Her tireless work and constant encouragement has made all the difference. Without her this book would never have been written!

Thanks to my wonderful congregation and the leadership of Calvary Baptist Church in New York City who have encouraged me and given me the time to think, study and write this book. To Bob Chancia and the Elders and Sam Jimenez and the Deacons—we experienced 9/11 together and God has made us stronger.

Thanks to my publisher, ANM, and Carl Gordon, Jay Temple and Alfonse Javed who believed in this project from the beginning and were a great help and encouragement to me. Thanks also to Betty Westmoreland and Brenda Thacker, my editors at ANM, who did a great job and often added a note of encouragement. A big thank you to Heather Kirk for a creative and beautifully designed book cover and layout!

A Time *for* Hope

Thanks to Craig Mader (#8), my brother-in-law, and to Brent Lewis, who God used over the years to challenge and convict me to write a book!

Thanks to my good friend John Gowling who offered some wonderful suggestions as he read my manuscript with a trained professional eye.

Thanks to George Anderson and Dave Shive who believed in me as a young Christian and gave me opportunities to use my gifts.

Thanks to my good friend, Dr. Erwin Lutzer, who was kind enough to offer a special endorsement for both myself and my book. His ministry at Moody Church is a powerful example of what a faithful and fruitful ministry looks like.

And a special thanks to my mom, Joan Epstein, who loves God and his Word and is a loving and fearless witness for Jesus Christ. Thank you for your love, prayers and encouragement—this book is also for you!

ABOUT THE AUTHOR

David Epstein grew up in a loving home and a confused world. He was a child of the 60's who was popular at school, talented academically and athletically, and received a number of major college scholarship offers. He loved Russian literature, philosophy, baseball and girls. He was also in despair. His search for meaning and purpose continually came up empty—leaving him angry, depressed and without hope. He tried to escape the debilitating emptiness with more learning, sex, alcohol and drugs. Nothing helped.

His entire family believed in God and had put their faith in Jesus Christ—but David had absolutely no interest. Nevertheless, his family and friends prayed for him continually.

He read deeply in science, literature, history, philosophy and religion—and one day decided to finally read the Bible. One night he was reading in Romans 5 where it says:

> You see, at just the right time, when we were still *powerless*, Christ died for the *ungodly*. Very rarely will anyone die for a righteous person, though for a good person someone might possibly dare to die. *But God demonstrates his own love for us* in this: While we were still *sinners*, Christ died for us. Since we have now been justified by his blood, how much more shall we

be saved from God's wrath through him! For if, while we were God's **enemies**, we were reconciled to him through the death of his Son, how much more, having been reconciled, shall we be saved through his life! Not only is this so, but we also boast in God through our Lord Jesus Christ, through whom we have now received reconciliation. (vs 6-11)

The truth overwhelmed him. He realized he was powerless, ungodly, sinful and an enemy of God. God's presence and love was overpowering, and David found himself on his face confessing his sins and asking God for forgiveness. When he finally stood up he was a new man—a follower of Jesus Christ.

God led him to study at Washington Bible College and Capital Bible Seminary, with further doctoral studies at Catholic University and the University of Maryland. He served on the faculty of Washington Bible College for eight years as an assistant professor of Biblical Studies and History. He also served as the assistant pastor at Mount Oak Methodist Church in Maryland and later as the senior pastor of the Metropolitan Bible Church and Forward Baptist Church in Canada.

In 1997, David was called by God to become the senior pastor of the historic Calvary Baptist Church in New York City, formerly pastored by Dr. Stephen Olford, Dr. Donald Hubbard, and Reverend James Rose.

David is blessed with his wife, Sandy, and his three children, Joshua, Jason, and Lindsay, and eight beautiful grandchildren.

Calvary Baptist Church continues to engage New York City and impact the world with the message of Jesus Christ.